The Meek Mountaineer

Fred Jacobson on the summit of the Allalinhorn

The Meek Mountaineer

A Climber's Armchair Companion

by FREDERICK L. JACOBSON

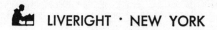 LIVERIGHT · NEW YORK

LIVERIGHT
386 Park Avenue South, New York, New York 10016

1.987654321
International Standard Book Number: 0-87140-584-9
Library of Congress Catalog Card Number: 73-93127

Manufactured in the United States of America

*This book is dedicated to the memory of Benny Perren,
who taught me how to climb the high peaks, and to Rony
Inderbinen, very much alive, in whose excellent company
I have reached so many of their summits.*

Acknowledgments

I should like to thank Sharon Novotny, Lisa Finlay, and Josephine Mansell, all of the European Camp Association, for their assistance in the typing of the manuscript. And special thanks go to John Morton for giving his blessing to them to spend their occasional free moments on this project. My gratitude also goes to Fern McNerney, whom I was fortunate to work with for two happy years, who was of invaluable assistance. And to Marie-Thérèse Furrer for her professional help.

Most important of all, I should like to express my appreciation to Margot Schutt, without whose support, editorial advice, and encouragement, this book could still be looking for a publisher. Thanks, too, to Christina Gottleib, the catalyst who put it all together.

Contents

Illustrations

Introduction

In this book, I hope to dispel the myth that mountaineering is a sport to be enjoyed only by supermen, fanatics, and acrobats. Certainly, to attain a top ranking one must develop acrobatic skills, a quality of fearlessness, unusual self-discipline, extraordinary stamina—all of these qualities and more. However, just as tennis isn't limited to the Rod Lavers and Ken Rosewalls, as Arnold Palmer does not typify the weekend golfer, as skiing can be enjoyed by those who are by no means Jean-Claude Killy, so, too, there is a large "middle ground" in climbing.

Consider the following letter from a climbing novice:

Dear Mom and Dad:

Yesterday morning at 9:30 A.M. I stood on the summit of the Matterhorn. As you know, this has been a lifelong dream for me, and there is much to tell you. First of all, let me assure you that I shall never climb again.

The whole thing was like a nightmare. About halfway up I thought I would quit. My heart was pounding, I had great difficulty breathing, a terrible headache, and some dizziness. My guide gave me three different pills plus a pep talk which together kept me going . . .

Our brief half-hour on top was spoiled by dense clouds which blocked out what I am told is a beautiful view. On the way down, it actually snowed, making the already difficult rocks considerably harder. I'm afraid I really lost my nerve . . .

On top of all this, the blisters on my heels started to bleed and were really quite painful . . .

The confessions of a superman? Hardly. They are, rather, the youthful confidences of the author at age twenty, shared with his worried parents. What makes this letter interesting is the fact that since then I have made no less than a dozen trips to the Swiss Alps to prolong these "nightmares."

It is my hope to convince the reader that mountaineering may be enjoyed on many levels, by people of widely differing abilities. Between the rocks that all of us scrambled up as children and Mount Everest, the summit of the world, lie peaks of every description—high and low, difficult and easy, nearly inaccessible and a few yards from civilization.

The late George Leigh-Mallory, last seen climbing into the summit mists of Mount Everest in 1924, once said: "Have we vanquished an enemy? None but ourselves." In an age of affluence, all of us need to push ourselves a little, to discover our limits, and to find our true identities. With the tremendous—and somewhat equalizing—impact of the communications media on our intellectual development, more and more people are extending their physical selves. "Back to nature," "physical fitness," "your own thing," "organic food"—all these concepts relate, in part, to the growing awareness of our physical selves.

Many books about mountain climbing have been written by famous climbers who have accomplished extraordinary feats. I am an unknown climber who has accomplished nothing extraordinary. However, I have spent parts of thirteen of the past fourteen summers in the High Alps; numerous weekends have been dedicated to climbing up and skiing down Mount Washington; countless hiking trips in Vermont, New Hampshire, and New York have provided a quality of living not easily measured. One spring, my closest friend and I crossed the Alps on skis— a seventy-mile pilgrimage through some of the grandest scenery in the world. A common denominator found in all of these endeavors—joy!

If the reader can vicariously share this joy and if he is moved to seek it on his own, this book will have served its purpose. For myself, I have found that mountain climbing leads to self-discovery. The important thing is to start slowly, to develop respect for the mountains, to know your own limits and—above all else—to enjoy yourself.

After twelve years of toil in the world of finance, I took a three-month leave of absence to write this book and to share some of my experiences with those people who are looking to the heights. Those who wish a technical work on the intricacies of pitonnage, belaying, double-rope technique, etc., should look elsewhere. For those who want to get started—or who wish to share pleasant reminiscences—I offer at least one approach that works.

Read on, and happy climbing!

Chapter 1

Molehills and
Other Miniatures

A step to the right. A long stretch. Careful with the foot. It's slipping. Ah! There's a good handhold. A quick pull up, feet scrambling against the smooth rock and then —the top!

The grass was not greener in the yard next door, but they did have a boulder—fifteen feet from base to summit —and it was there that my earliest mountain fantasies were acted out. The boulder had one face that overhung. I avoided it then, even as I avoid the hardest routes today. But the other three faces presented ample opportunities for a ten-year-old to test himself. One was a broken slab, the second had a little crack, and the third a ridge running up it. Through endless repetitions, I became quite proficient at the three routes, even putting in a few variants. I was no rock engineer, but an enthusiast nevertheless.

As a matter of fact, my climbing experience went back even further. At age four, I climbed the locally famous Sunset Hill, near Lake Dunmore in Vermont, a tree-covered giant some two hundred feet high. I was fortunate in coming from a long line of nature lovers— horseback riders, skiers, hikers, gardeners. The first fifteen summers of my life were spent in the Green Mountain

hills of Vermont, where my family had a summer home on
Lake Dunmore, eight miles south of Middlebury. Since
1930, my grandparents had run a children's summer camp
on the lake. And I remember longing—even at age two
and three—to be part of the group of young boys who
swam and sailed and hiked together all day. The summer
I turned five my dreams were realized. As a "freshman,"
my horizons widened—a walk to the fish hatcheries, a
cookout at nearby Texas Falls, and finally a trip up Sunset
Hill. Almost thirty years have blurred many details of that
climb, but I still remember the thrill of stepping off the
road and setting out in the woods. I remember the open
fields, with the wild berries, and chipmunks, a jack-in-the-
pulpit. Even that young, I sensed the mystery of seeking
out the unknown. As we neared the summit of Sunset Hill,
I felt a strange dichotomy (though I didn't know the word
at that time!): on the one hand, I was realizing a dream;
on the other, I was losing it. Years later, I was to experience a deeper but similar feeling on the Matterhorn. I
remember also the view from the summit of that first
climb, and that I felt closer to the campers who'd come
with me on this adventure.

I remained a freshman, condemned to go no higher
than Sunset Hill for two more summers. I had already
raised my sights to Moosalamoo, the mountain towering
more than a thousand feet above the lake, but there was
no sense of urgency. I knew that in time I would be old
enough and then I would have my chance. Meanwhile I
set out to become expert on Sunset Hill.

There were also trips to the Cascades, a beautiful
series of waterfalls with a swimming hole where I still
love to swim, and to Bald Hill, a gentle peak to the north
of the lake heavily populated by some not so gentle red
ants. Finally, the summer I turned eight, there was a trip
to Moosalamoo, up to Rattlesnake Point via the Deer

Trail. Each step of the way remains firmly fixed in my mind, aided perhaps by the fact that I have since repeated the ascent some hundred times—as camper, as counselor, with friends, alone, in training, after a summer of Alpine climbing, in fair weather and foul. Today it is hard to remember the "difficulties," but it was a big climb then—an all-day effort rather than the pre-breakfast warmup it later became.

First a road through the woods. Then an open meadow, a brook, and the road narrowed to a footpath. Up through pine and oak, through huge boulders and finally to the Deer's Staircase. It was steep, and as we crawled along the ledge I felt fear for the first time in the mountains, in this case caused by the "exposure"* of a ten-foot drop. Years later, of course, I would sense the same fear more intensely.

Above the Staircase was General's Lookout, with a magnificent view of the lake. Then followed a steep section—Waboo's Workout—and then Major's Lookout. Above, a beautiful traverse through a pine forest, the path covered with a cushion of pine needles. Up Slim's Slide to a crawl through the Narrow Gauge—a huge slab leaning against the cliffs of Rattlesnake Point, which soar above. Finally, along the base of the cliffs and up a short scramble to the Point. This was a real climb and I could scarcely conceal my excitement. That evening, as the setting sun shone on the high cliffs, I could hardly believe that I had stood there only a few hours earlier.

At age ten, my first "famous" summit was climbed—Mount Mansfield, more famous now for its skiing challenge. This was the highest peak in Vermont, a peak I had seen a year earlier when I was permitted to accompany an older group to its base. Mount Mansfield was three thou-

* Exposure relates to the space beneath your feet. The farther down it is to terra firma, the more exposed a place is said to be.

sand feet above the Smuggler's Notch road. To put this in perspective, the Matterhorn itself rises four thousand feet above its base hut. Needless to say, the nature of the climbing is altogether different, but the vertical feet involved in climbing Mount Mansfield are considerable.

Standing at the foot of the peak, I experienced doubt for the first time. The mountain could be climbed; many had done it. But would I be able to make it? There are those who need to discover, who need to set foot where no man has ventured before. At age five—and today—I find great satisfaction in setting foot where others may have ventured but I have never been. We had sleeping bags—this was our first overnight trip—and the extra weight added to my anxiety. This was hard work, but I told myself that it was just as hard for my campmates, harder for most of them, who were smaller than I. There must be a degree of masochism in all of us, which is simply intensified in hikers and climbers. But I felt a certain strength in being able to adjust to the discomfort and overcome it. Labored breathing could be regulated once a comfortable pace was established. Self-confidence rises as challenges are met successfully. But I'm getting ahead of myself! As a ten-year-old, I was determined not to complain, not to show weakness. I concentrated on keeping up, and tried to stay at the front. We camped out at Taft Lodge—about a thousand feet below the highest summit—without major incident although our camp became the target for some hungry porcupines, and we completed the climb next day. The air was cleaner. The valley shrank below us, and for the first time in my life I emerged above the treeline. As we rose above Eagle Pass to the summit—the Chin—a remarkable thing happened. One of our counselors—an all-American football player whose name will go unrecorded here—became frightened and would go no

The summit of Mount Mansfield in winter

farther. It was hard to believe, but I realized then that mountains were not for everyone—for mortals yes, but not for mortals with acrophobia!

On the summit, those of us who had persevered (about half had dropped out) enjoyed a rare moment. The world was spread beneath our feet. If the White Mountains rose higher to the east, we did not feel their presence. To the west lay Lake Champlain, and all around us endless ranges of hills, gentle and beckoning. I wanted to know all of them, to see the world from their summits even as I then could see it from Mount Mansfield.

I still prefer to take one area and know it intimately rather than make a climb or two and then seek out other valleys. I have climbed the thirty-four trails that cover Mount Mansfield. I have traversed the mountain from north to south, from east to west (and the reverse directions), sometimes twice in one day. I have slept in its lodges, in tents, under the stars on one of its summits. A few years ago, I was leading a friend of mine and his wife on a Memorial Day traverse. Coming down from the Chin, we were surprised by several feet of snow still lying in the woods. Having wandered some ten feet from the marked trail, I have lost the privilege of saying that I know the mountain like the back of my hand! I remember that first climb up Mount Mansfield as one of the turning points in my life.

An even more important event took place the same summer. It was not another climb, it was a motion picture called *The Challenge* based on the first climbing of the Matterhorn. From the moment I saw the actors playing the parts of Edward C. Whymper and Jean-Antoine Carrel crawling up the slopes of the huge mountain, my life was changed. My dreams were filled with mountains from then on. As soon as I got home, I started borrowing books on mountain climbing from the library. In later years, I bought climbing books, and now my collection numbers some five hundred volumes. Whymper's *Scrambles Amongst the Alps*, A. F. Mummery's *My Climbs in the Alps and Caucasus*, Leslie Stephen's *The Playground of Europe*, John Tyndall's *Hours of Exercise in the Alps*, and, most important, the numerous works of Frank Smythe formed the backbone of my armchair climbing education. Climbers were my heroes. My parents took me to a lecture by Maurice Herzog, leader of the successful Annapurna expedition—the first eight-thousand-meter peak to be climbed. I scanned newspapers with new interest, in the unlikely event that there might be mountaineering news.

However, from age ten to twenty, nothing new was added to my mountain repertory. I grew, of course, and as my stride lengthened, the times required to climb the familiar peaks in Vermont decreased. In camp I had established myself as one of the "hiking elite," capable of carrying the heaviest loads without complaining. Then I became a counselor, a hiking leader on Vermont's trails.

Climbing, as opposed to hiking, requires the use of a rope to protect the climber from possible injuries in the event of a slip. I had not yet aspired to being a member of the climbing fraternity; my climbing was done vicariously through the printed word. After all, mountain climbing with ropes was the special domain of Swiss guides and their equally hearty fellow Europeans. Books like Elizabeth Knowlton's *The Naked Mountain* had made me aware that there were some American climbers, but in the early 1950s, the Westchester suburbs of New York City had produced few of them. There was no one to talk to about my dreams. Such names as Hans Kraus and Fritz Weissner were legends, but legends didn't often stoop to talk to mortals. I was a strong hiker, but climbing seemed an altogether different undertaking.

In March 1959 things changed.

Through my first three years at Yale, I was less and less interested in physical fitness. On my own for the first time, pool, Ping-Pong, billiards, and drinking formed my daily routine. Even my mountain reading trailed off, as reading for my courses took up all my time, keeping me busier than I would have liked. However, in March of 1959 a high-school friend and I started to plan our itinerary for a European "grand tour."

We had little trouble agreeing on London, Paris, Munich, Vienna, Venice, Florence, and Cap d'Antibes. My friend wanted to visit his childhood governess, who had returned to her native Germany. I appreciated but did not share his enthusiasm for this project. He planned to go north from Zurich. I decided that I would go south—to Zermatt! And I wrote a letter to the president of the Zermatt Guides:

Dear Sir:

I plan to be in Zermatt July 7–16 and would like to climb the Matterhorn. I have already climbed Mount Mansfield many times and feel I am prepared. Please write me if this is all right.

The letter was answered courteously—and affirmatively— by Perren Gottlieb, who was the leader of the Zermatt Guides. As the school days ran out, I got more and more excited about my European trip, and though I didn't really think I would do the Matterhorn, I reasoned that it would be fun to do some good hikes and perhaps, if all went well, set foot on the mountain.

The mountain was in good shape that year, but I—not surprisingly—was not. Sailing over on the *Queen Elizabeth*, my friend and I had met two delightful girls from Wheeling, West Virginia. Being good sports, they agreed to play bridge with us for one drink per person per rubber. Five and a half days later, undefeated, I walked off the ship ninety drinks heavier (my friend had kept and counted my swizzle sticks). Later, some twenty pounds overweight, I arrived in Zurich. The next day I embarked for Brig, where one changes to the little red train that climbs up to Zermatt.

As the train passed through Thun, Spiez, and Kandersteg, I gazed at breathtaking views of the Bernese Alps. Although I had read many books and seen much photography, I was quite unprepared for the magnificence of the eternal snows. Finally, after the long traverse through Loetschberg down to Brig, the train threaded its way up the Zermatt valley. I glimpsed signs for the names I knew only through my books. Visp, Stalden, St. Niklaus—home of a generation of great guides—Burgener, Knubel, Lochmatter. Randa followed, and Täsch, and finally Zermatt. The years have since enabled me to name the many high peaks that reveal themselves in part as the train winds through the valley; but that first time I was only aware of drawing nearer and nearer to the Matterhorn, which I thought was the highest peak in the area (actually five are higher).

In Zermatt I walked up the main street (at that time the only one!) to my hotel, the Tannenhof. On the balcony, I turned around and saw it—the Matterhorn! It took a full fifteen minutes before I came back to earth, went up to my room, and unpacked.

The first order of business was to search out Perren Gottlieb. I was told that he was in the mountains, but that his brother Bernard was in town. After an hour of asking for Bernard Gottlieb and getting no response, I finally discovered that the Swiss put the family name first. It was hardly surprising that no one had heard of Bernard Gottlieb, but the name Perren Bernard brought immediate recognition.

From the moment I shook hands with Benny Perren, I liked him and knew that I would have complete confidence in him. He was a short, stocky man, perhaps five feet seven. He had powerful arms and legs, blond hair, and piercing blue eyes. I only realized later that I had had the good fortune to meet up with one of Zermatt's truly great guides. I learned from others that Benny had been the Swiss downhill champion, a sure candidate for the 1952 Olympics until he broke his leg in Wengen. Today, fourteen years after our first meeting, his legend lives and grows.

But for that moment, a twenty-year-old boy had made a new friend, had met a hero. Benny took me to the various shops to buy the equipment I would need—boots, knickers, glacier goggles, crampons, ice ax, rucksack—and explained the use of each item. The boots had special cleated soles to adhere to the rocks. The crampons were iron spikes strapped to the boots to make it possible to climb over ice and hard snow. The ice ax was used for balance, for chopping steps in the ice, for probing crevasses, or to stop yourself in case of a slip on steep snow. We had a beer together and he traced out several "walks" for me which, he said, would be good training for the more serious business of climbing.

Benny said he would take me on the Riffelhorn in three or four days, where I could get some practice and he could determine whether it would be feasible to take me up the Matterhorn. If not, he would take me up the Breithorn, another four-thousand-meter peak, but a simple snow peak with no rock climbing.

The next morning I decided to walk to the Hörnli Hut, the cabin that lies at the foot of the so-called tourist route on the Matterhorn.

There are several hundred huts spread throughout the Alps. There are two basic types: the mountain hut, generally run by the Alpine Club of the country involved; and the mountain hotel, generally privately owned and run for profit.

In Switzerland, the Swiss Alpine Club is responsible for the running of more than one hundred mountain huts. These huts all provide sleeping accommodations, generally dortoirs, for between twenty and one hundred and twenty climbers. The larger huts generally have a guardian or staff which provides hot food and beverages for those who do not bring their own rations.

The cost of lodging is about three dollars, although members of the Swiss Alpine Club and clubs with reciprocal arrangements are entitled to a fifty-percent discount. With breakfast, dinner, taxes, and wood included, one should allow twelve to fifteen dollars per day at a hut.

From these huts, virtually every high peak in Switzerland may be climbed in a single day. Often, climbers may descend all the way down to the nearest village in the valley, rather than spending an additional night at the hut. If a series of climbs are planned, longer stays at the hut are possible.

The huts are open to the public, although members of the Swiss Alpine Club have first priority (which can be important in high season), and certain rooms within the huts are reserved for the exclusive use of club members.

Trying to do as the Romans, I bought a bottle of wine, some bread and cheese, and chocolate. Armed with these provisions I set off for my "walk," a climb of more than five thousand feet, a difference in elevation almost twice as great as Mount Mansfield from base to summit. It was soon obvious to me that this walk would be quite a test. Unaccustomed to the altitude—at 5500 feet Zermatt is considerably higher than the summit of Mount Mansfield—I set too fast a pace for myself. In no time at all, I was drenched with perspiration and decided to lighten my

load. The wine was regretfully jettisoned and the hike re-
sumed. A little farther on, I was overcome by the odor of
the strong local cheese, and it, too, was cast off. At
Schwarzsee—the halfway point—I decided to nibble on
some bread. To my great disappointment, the lady in the
store had done me a great favor and smothered the bread
with an inedible mustard. More jetsam! Finally, beneath
the hut, my energy flagging, I decided to get some quick
energy from the chocolate. Failure again. Too close to my
overheated body, it had liquefied, and it dribbled to the
ground when I opened the wrapper!

The hike had been straightforward, with no dangerous places or unreasonable exposure, but I was finished.
When I reached the hut I threw myself on a bench, caus-
ing considerable alarm. I knew enough German to understand that the consensus was that I had probably suffered
a heart attack. I smiled weakly, mumbled, *"Alles gute,"*
and had a bowl of soup.

When I was sufficiently recovered, I looked around
. . . and up. I had heard expert climbers refer to the
Matterhorn as a "walk." One look was enough to assure
me that I would never "walk" here. For close to a vertical
mile, the mountain rises in soaring steps, tremendous cliffs,
and precipices dwarfing anything I had known before.

Somewhat discouraged, I started down. The climbers
stayed at the hut, and I was alone on my way back to
Schwarzsee. Not quite alone. I was delighted to see a
flock of sheep and goats grazing, but my delight waned
considerably when these wild creatures attacked me. They
butted me from behind, and every time I turned my back
I found myself speeded on my way. Nothing painful, but
where the path narrowed, there was cause for concern.
Finally I descended backward and was left in trembling
peace. I should hasten to assure the reader that today's
goats and sheep are far friendlier, supervised by a benev-
olent Zermatt tourist bureau.

About this time, I realized that my boots were pinching me and that my heels were already quite sore. By the time I reached the village at sundown, I was dragging myself along. I learned later that new boots must be broken in slowly. That night I slept poorly. Somehow a fly had entered my ear and buzzed all night. In the morning I asked for a doctor, but when he examined me, no fly could be found. Relieved that no surgery would be necessary, I learned that I was merely suffering from the altitude and would be fine in a couple of days.

There were several other long "walks," and by the time Benny and I set off for the Riffelhorn, I was suffering from heel blisters that were raw to the point of bleeding. Despite the best healing powders the doctors of Zermatt, Garmisch, Innsbruck, Salzburg, and Vienna could provide, it was three months before I had healed heels!

The Riffelhorn started well enough. I can still remember the thrill of tying on the rope for the first time. I still experience a somewhat mystical feeling in tying myself and my life to a climbing companion. From the "Seeseite," we climbed up above the Riffelsee. I was hardly graceful, but I managed the milder pitches and was not unduly aware of the exposure. A pitch—usually between 30 to 150 feet—is the climbing distance from the leader's initial move to where he stops to bring up the next man. We got to the top in short order—it seemed like less than an hour, although it may have been more. It all seemed too easy. I had shaken Benny's hand, pleased that we had conquered our first peak together. I thought it was a little early for lunch, but was hardly ready for what followed. Benny told me to go down the other side—the "glacier side" of the mountain. I walked to the edge of what appeared to be a vertical precipice.

"Which way, Benny?"

"Down!"

"I understand that, but do I go left or right first?"

"Down."

"But which way, Benny?"

"Straight down, now."

I couldn't believe it. Here was a precipice vastly more dangerous than the Deer's Staircase—it was steeper and smoother, and thousands of feet of air lay between me and the Gorner Glacier below. Now my climbing lesson began in earnest. Benny was decisive, sure-footed, and steady of nerve. All three qualities were notably absent in my efforts. "Lean away from the rock." "Face out when you climb down, or sideways." "Only face in when it is very steep." "Take small steps." "Put your boots flat on the rock." "Not too much with the arms." The fact that my hands and feet still clung to the mountain meant that I must be doing something right, but I couldn't for the life of me think what it was. Benny's comments were gentle but firm. Unlike many other sports, climbing demands continuous technical correctness. You can't be "out of control" for even a moment. Unlike skiing, you can't just sit down when things seem to be getting out of hand. Benny explained the rationale behind each instruction. It all made sense, but my body would not always obey my mind's commands. The exposure was frightening to say the least.

People who don't climb think that all serious climbing is vertical. Certainly rock specialists such as the Yosemite climbers are very much at home in the world of the vertical. But there are great challenges that fall considerably short of ninety degrees. Imagine a steep staircase you've climbed. If you were to put this staircase on top of the Empire State Building, it would seem steeper and you would exercise considerably more care in climbing it. If you were then to remove the banister, you would feel even less secure and might resort to crawling on your hands and knees, even though this would not be necessary, nor help you to climb. Finally, think of the staircase being coated with ice. As you can imagine, slabs need be neither vertical nor smooth to require a healthy respect.

I developed a healthy respect for the Riffelhorn that day. We climbed down an open corner, the Gletscher Ecke, and then back up the Gletscher Couloir, a steep gully with less exposure. Finally down the Skyline Ridge, I learned to rappell, or down-rope.* By wrapping the rope around myself as Benny instructed I was able to lower myself through space, dropping beneath a cliff that I could never have climbed down. And by the end of the day I had learned quite a lot—that little hand- and footholds could be used, that the boot should be placed flat against the rock, and that leaning out and away from the rock helped to keep the boots flat. Most important, I learned that it was comforting (and when technique failed, essential!) to have a tight rope from above. There were slips, but somehow my life never seemed to be in danger.

Despite this, my nerves were frayed by the tension of the preceding hours. Benny, ignoring my mental exhaustion, declared the day a success. We could climb the Matterhorn in three or four days!

---

* Rappelling—a controlled slide (friction of hands, legs, and body against rope) down a doubled rope which is securely fixed to an anchor above. The anchor could be a rock, outcrop, or a piton (screw) driven into the rock with a snap ring through it.

Chapter 2

The Matterhorn—
An End and a Beginning

I took yet another "walk" for Matterhorn preparation —this time up the 11,500-foot Mettelhorn—which entailed an ascent of six thousand vertical feet above Zermatt and proved that with enough dressings and bandages I could walk despite my heels.

I also did considerably more mental preparation. I saw a film entitled *Whymper's Way to the Matterhorn*, in which a young American girl, Christine Allen, followed in the footsteps of the first conqueror of the mountain. Although it was fully a decade before the beginning of the Women's Liberation movement, I decided that this girl was considerably more than equal. She was fearless! I, in turn, got gooseflesh just watching the film. My confidence wavered. How could anyone look at that peak and think it easy? Furthermore, I visited the Alpine Museum and saw a rather extraordinary collection of rusted crampons, broken ropes, and mutilated climbing boots. These mementos of the Matterhorn reinforced my impression that this was no mountain to be taken lightly. Several hours in the cemetery, and I was ready to call off my attempt. Here, the tombstones recalled an incredible variety of appalling accidents. Weisshorn, Dent Blanche, Pollux, Lyskamm, Breithorn, Täschhorn—all had claimed their own victims. But the Matterhorn seemed to be the most implacable. Climbers of all ages and nationalities had perished on its slopes. I even noted some young Americans who had become its prey.

Each day I looked up at the peak with growing self-doubt. My confidence only returned in Benny's presence. My better judgment told me to leave it to the Swiss heroes. And yet my dreams of ten years beckoned, towered far above, in isolated splendor. I simply couldn't retreat without a good try. I knew I had to "rub my nose against the rock," and if, on close inspection, it was too much for me, we would turn back. Benny, straining my credulity, assured me there was nothing as difficult as what we had done on the Riffelhorn.

July 13 dawned bright and clear. My usually robust appetite deserted me. This was the day on which I was to set out for the immortal peak. About three o'clock that afternoon Benny met me at the Schwarzsee lift, which we took to the lake at the base of the Matterhorn. An easy two-hour walk by mule path brought us to the Hörnli Hut. Above, the mountain soared to infinite heights. Benny pointed out many of the other peaks, which gradually were bathed in that unique roseate light known as Alpenglow.

The hut was inhabited by a band of incredibly hardy guides and their clients, each of whom seemed tougher than the last. I felt quite out of place in their company. My spirits picked up when an American girl named Kathy entered the hut, but they were dashed again when I learned that she and her guide were planning to climb the Zmutt Ridge, a far harder climb than the "regular way." I was convinced that—myself excepted—there were no mortals in the hut. Self-conscious about my limited

ability to speak German and lesser ability to climb mountains, I was sure that every time they laughed they were
laughing at the bloated young American who was daring
to set foot on the hallowed mountain.

After dinner, I went to my room and tried to sleep.
At an altitude of almost eleven thousand feet and over-
stimulated as I was by visions of what the next day held
in store, sleep did not come easily. After what seemed
like hours, I was almost out when my roommate exploded
into the room. Clomping around in heavy boots, he barked
out his hearty German greetings. I tried *Gute nacht* softly
several times. The conversation ceased, but as he washed
himself, he virtually bellowed and crashed around the
room, ending all hopes of sleep. Outside the window, the
black silhouette of the mountain rose, dark and terrifying.
Until that night I had never had five minutes of insomnia,
yet as I lay there meditating on how important it was to
sleep, on how I would have to call on my deepest reservoirs
the next day, on the impossibility of a successful ascent
without adequate sleep, I was totally frustrated in my
efforts. I got up once to go to the bathroom, another time
to look at the weather, which I prayed would break. As
I stepped out alone into the starry night, I was engulfed
in a final wave of fear. And then, resigned to my fate, I
went back to bed. At two forty-five A.M., Benny appeared
to wish me good morning. This is a normal time to arise in
the mountains. Particularly when there is snow to be
climbed (the Matterhorn was quite "dry" that year), one
must climb early before the sun has softened the snow and
loosened the rocks. One climbs by headlight or—when
propitious—by moonlight.

Knowing how much I would need the energy, I was
totally unable to eat my breakfast. At three-thirty A.M. we
stepped out into the night. Already there were some
lanterns above us, eerie phantoms in the darkness. When

A "belay"

Benny tied the rope around me, I felt reassured. With
Benny there would be no problem. A few yards across
some snow, and we were at the foot of the first steep rocks.

It was electric—that first contact with the rock of the
Matterhorn. Ten years of reading, dreaming, planning—
and now we were under way. I wondered why the lights
above seemed to grow smaller. There was an embarrass-
ingly easy explanation—the other climbers were moving
faster than we were. But Benny didn't seem to mind. A
true guide, he enjoyed showing an appreciative amateur
the beauties of the mountains. We handled each pitch,
often climbing together. I would try to watch Benny's
movements and follow exactly in his footsteps. On the
steeper bits, he would go first, then bring in the rope,
keeping it taut between us to lessen the distance I might
fall in case of a slip (this is known as a "belay") as I
rejoined him on a more level platform. In this fashion we
made reasonable if not spectacular progress.

There was actually little climbing on the ridge itself.
Rather, we climbed the slabs of the east face. The climbing was nowhere difficult in the sense that acrobatic
agility or great muscular strength was required. On the
other hand, however, this was no "walk." The exposure,
naturally, increased the higher we rose. Occasionally we
would go up and over or around gendarmes, pinnacles of
rock striking out from the normal angle of the ridge that
"held up the traffic," and there I became increasingly
aware of the plunging depths on either side of the ridge.

After a couple of hours of such work, I noticed a
definite shortness of breath, a quickening of my pulse,
and a feeling of dizziness. Damn all those drinks on the
Queen Elizabeth. Future climbs taught me that altitude
sickness, while less extreme when one is in good shape,
cannot be altogether eliminated. It affects people differently at different altitudes.

In my case, on July 14, 1959, I began to suffer rather intensely at about 12,500 feet, some 2000 feet above the Hörnli Hut and 500 feet below the Solvay Hut, an emergency refuge just above the hardest part of the route—the Moseley Blatte (to digress, having a *blatte*, slab, named after you is worth avoiding. This honor is generally accorded posthumously to those who have failed fatally to negotiate the slab in question!).

I decided to play the stoic and not reveal my multiple problems. My act was altogether unsuccessful, as my turtle pace spoke louder than words. Benny produced three pills—one for each of my problems—and some warm tea. As this ceremony was being performed, I was treated to my first Alpine sunrise. The sky lightened in the east, and slowly the high peaks were bathed in warm sunlight. The summit of the Matterhorn turned gold, and this golden hue came down to meet us on our upward journey. We climbed slowly up and over the Moseley Blatte and scrambled into the Solvay Refuge. Then we clambered over the Upper Moseley Blatte and approached the shoulder of the mountain, meeting snow for the first time. The snow was firm but not icy, so we didn't need our crampons. We came to the fixed ropes, just below the "roof," that section, generally snowy, where the angle eases off to the summit. These help the climber up an otherwise difficult section. Forgetting my apprenticeship and ignoring the many footholds, I hauled myself up these ropes, using my arms alone. This is hard enough work at sea level; it was killing at about fourteen thousand feet. I emerged from the final rope, blowing like a giant fish out of the water. This was perhaps my most brilliant demonstration of how *not* to climb the Matterhorn.

Some steep snow slopes came next, then some less steep ones. Then I found myself exhilarated beyond words, for the ridge dipped slightly ahead of me, before rising to

Fred Jacobson at close to 13,000 feet on the Matterhorn

the cross on the Italian summit. We had reached the top!

I was incredulous. Eleven years earlier I had seen *The Challenge* and felt my own challenge. Endless hours of reading, imagining, romanticizing well beyond the limits of reality—and now the summit was beneath my feet! I was glad my dark glasses concealed my involuntary tears. Dreams are not necessarily meant to be realized. In the realization you lose the dream, and new dreams are not always easily found. The world lay beneath our feet—a world far vaster and more awesome than the one I'd seen from Mount Mansfield eleven years earlier.

We didn't say much, Benny and I, each lost in our private thoughts. I was exhausted, but rallied myself sufficiently to pose for a summit picture. Benny started to name the surrounding peaks for me. He began—and ended —with the nearby Dent Blanche. No sooner had my lesson begun than ominous clouds swirled up from below. Without further ado, we started down. Facing out on the gentle roof, I had my first real glimpse of exposure. Coming up, I had looked five to ten feet in front of me, studying where I would step next. Now, facing out, the entire mountain dropped away from me, the appalling north face on my left and on the right the east face, whose upper portion appears to overhang! All of a sudden I felt the same fear I had experienced when Benny told me to descend the steep side of the Riffelhorn. I started down falteringly. At the fixed ropes, I virtually slid down, fear and exhaustion leading me once again to overlook the footholds. At the bottom of the ropes, a new problem developed: it began to snow. Rock that was easy when dry became increasingly slippery as the snow fell. I also became aware that my heels, despite careful bandaging, had opened up once again. I now resorted to the five-pointed descent—two hands, two feet, and a very tight rope from behind. This is considered the ultimate in bad form—for the guide and the tourist—and our mutual shame was minimized only because most of the other climbers were well ahead of us and couldn't witness my collapse.

Benny made several polite suggestions that I quite literally "get off my ass." Once he sensed the extent of my physical and mental deterioration, he left me to my own devices. Several times I slipped and my weight dragged on the rope, held carefully by my guide. With such nervous baggage for a ropemate, Benny must have felt his own nerves somewhat frazzled by the time we regained the hut. The Solvay Hut, the Moseley Blatte, the crest, the slabs—all in reverse—and finally the ordeal was ended.

The normal time is five hours up, three and a half down. We had been six hours each way. Benny must have had to swallow hard as he offered his congratulations.

A final humorous note. At the Hörnli Hut, I removed my boots and changed into sneakers. To be helpful, Benny offered to carry one of my boots down to Schwarzsee. Since the path was easy and there was no danger, Benny ran ahead. Who knows how many people climbing up to the hut that afternoon thought the Matterhorn had been the scene of another ghastly accident when they saw Benny with the single boot? Countless expressions of relief greeted me as I appeared some ten minutes behind him on the trail—with the other boot. Back in the village, Benny walked me to my hotel and again congratulated me. At the hotel, where most of the residents were walkers rather than climbers, I was given a hero's greeting at dinner. I couldn't respond as I wanted to. I was too tired to eat. Having guzzled two quarts of various nonalcoholic liquids, I waved a hero's farewell to the company assembled in the dining room and made my way to my room.

I awoke at six o'clock the following evening. I met Benny for a beer and he presented me with a certificate, as official recognition of my accomplishment. That night I wrote the despairing letter that appears in the introduction. Many adventuresome young Americans come to Zermatt to "do" the Matterhorn, generally as unprepared as I had been. The climb usually marks their first and last ascent. When I left on the sixteenth, I had no reason to suspect that I would stray from the usual "first and last climb" pattern. However, I had a feeling I would *somehow* see my new friend again.

When I got home after the rest of the grand tour, my family and friends looked with admiration at the few slides I had managed to take on the Matterhorn. The fears

grew dim, the blisters healed, the fatigue was forgotten.
By November my competitive spirit was back. I knew I
had not climbed well. Why not go back and improve to
the point where I could truly enjoy the climb, I wondered.
Or perhaps try another mountain? Or at least see Benny
again?

My father didn't entirely approve of a second grand
tour. I would be graduating from college and would be on
my own. If I wanted to return to Europe, I would have to
earn my way. So, during my senior year, I typed papers
for fellow students, sold magazines, sold gifts at Christmas,
shoveled snow during the winter, and washed cars with a
frenzy. My father helped me to secure free passage on a
freighter. Still short of funds, I sold my stamp collection.

I graduated from Yale on a Monday. On Tuesday I
set sail for Paris, Geneva, and Matterhorn country!

Paris was fun, Geneva interesting. But after two
weeks, I headed back to Zermatt, eager to come to grips
once more with the mountains. It was late June. Back at
the Tannenhof, I unpacked my equipment and looked for
Benny. Yes, he would be happy to climb with me again
and was sure that with practice I would improve.

After the now-familiar training walks, we set out for
the Breithorn—a snow hike rather than a real climb—but
good for purposes of acclimatization. We walked across the
easy Theodul Glacier to the Gandegg Hut, had an early
dinner, and went to bed. When we awoke at three o'clock,
it was snowing—an omen of things to come in the summer
of 1960. We returned to Zermatt, where we waited for
better weather. On our second try, things went better.
Since the Breithorn is Zermatt's easiest four-thousand-
meter peak, there were no climbing difficulties, although
I slowed up a bit at the top. The view—this time unim-
peded by storm clouds—was extraordinary. To the south,

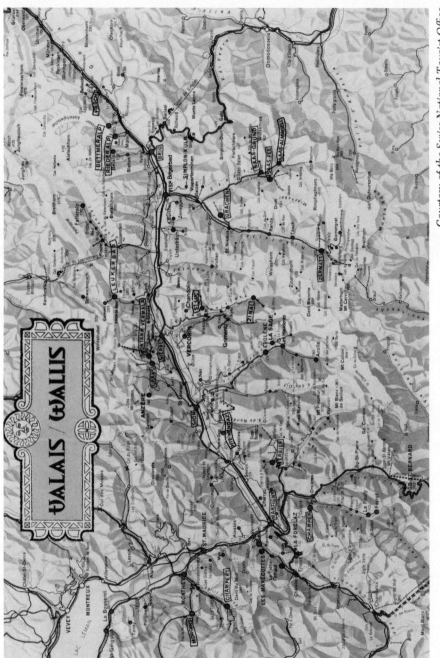

the Italian Alps were ranged peak after peak, the Grivola and the Gran Paradiso in the middle ground, and the Monte Viso in the distant background. To the east were Castor, Pollux, Lyskamm, and Monte Rosa. To the west rose the Matterhorn itself, with Mont Blanc—sixty miles away—and Grand Combin, Dent d'Hérens, Dent Blanche, Obergabelhorn, and Wellenkuppe. To the north we could see the crenellated ridges of the Zinal Rothorn and Weisshorn on the left and the Saas peaks—Adlerhorn, Strahlhorn, Rimpfischhorn, Allalin, Alphubel, Täschhorn, Dom, Sudlenz, Nadelgrat, and the northernmost Dürrenhorn—on the right. In summers to come, I grew more and more familiar with most of these peaks, but in July 1960 they seemed a mysterious new world to me—peak after peak, each with its own distinctive shape. Benny patiently named each one for me, as well as the passes that wound between.

On the way down I began to suffer from Benny's training regime. We had deliberately brought nothing to drink—"to help toughen you," in Benny's words. I may have toughened mentally, but by the time we returned to Gandegg, my throat was raw. It was a small price to pay, however, for my first four-thousand-meter peak of the summer.

As the snows continued to linger on the higher peaks, we shifted to the Saas Valley, in particular to Saas Grund and the Weissmies Hut above it. Our plan was to climb the Jägigrat, a spiky rock ridge that rises to only 3500 meters. This climb taught me that getting to the top does not necessarily mean an end to the hard climbing.

The walk up to the Weissmies Hut is not very strenuous, and it is particularly beautiful—a rewarding combination. We walked up slowly through the woods and on to the pasturelands of Triftalp, then across several mountain streams and past numerous shepherds' huts to the hut itself.

An amusing incident followed. There were three very attractive Austrian girls who were planning to make the same climb with three of the Julen brothers of Zermatt. My comment on their beauty brought a rather unexpected suggestion from Benny.

"After dinner, why don't you take one of them to bed with you."

"Benny, you've got to be kidding!"

"No, no, here in the huts it's quite all right."

It was true that in the mountain huts of the Swiss Alpine Club, all climbers shared a common dormitory with narrow mattresses, tiny pillows, and blankets available on a first-come, first-served basis. However, being *next* to someone and *with* someone were two quite different propositions.

"Benny, I don't even know those girls. How could I?"

"Well, not too long, for that can be quite tiring at high altitudes. But just for a little while calms the nerves. You'll climb better."

I swallowed my surprise.

In 1960, at my naïve stage of development, "free love" was one of the hidden pleasures of Europe. My friends and I at college had often discussed the finer points of this liberal system. In short, the consensus was that you saw someone attractive, indicated your desire, and were immediately invited to satisfy that desire—"for free." Still, free love in the mountain huts of Switzerland?

"I'll arrange everything," said Benny.

"Benny, you're just joking, right?" I wanted to believe him.

Most of the dinner conversation centered on the proposed Alpine "love-in." If my gullibility was extreme, you must remember that Benny was my oracle for all Alpine matters. I remained skeptical until after dinner. Benny lay down in a corner of the bunkroom, and I next to him. When the three Austrian girls slipped into their long johns and lay down beside me, I began to lose my doubts. Benny was right again!

However, caution was still the watchword. Pretending to be asleep, I slowly moved my right hand toward the nearest Austrian "peak." Each time I did so, I tossed in my feigned sleep, let out a snore/groan, and inched closer. Finally the objective was cupped gently. There was no particular reaction. My confidence rose—and my belief in Benny's knowledge and *savoir faire* in the mountains with it. Spirits soaring, I moved my hand sharply downward. Before it could quite reach its objective, Austrian fury was unleashed.

"What the hell do you think you are doing?"

The words rang out loudly in a room long quiet. Most of the other climbers had been sleeping or on the verge of sleep when the violated Brünhilde's trumpet cry rent the air. Immediately, countless flashlights were pointed in my direction, accompanied by a crescendo of German expletives. I assumed a fetal position under my blanket, trembling with fear lest I be asked to sleep outside. Benny was shaking too, not from fear, but uncontrollable amusement. When the commotion had subsided, I gave Benny a firm elbow in the ribs and tried as best I could to sleep surrounded by hostile Austrian peaks and a company of Germanic enemies! At breakfast, one of the Julens asked how the girls had slept. The offended one gave me an icy stare and replied "not so good." With this trauma behind me, we proceeded to the climb.

The climb up the mountain the next morning was straightforward enough. However, once we were on the ridge, the real problems started, the biggest of which was that this was my first rock climb of the season, and it was too hard for me. The ridge was a series of towers and sharp edges. On the sharpest parts of the ridge, Benny would walk along as though he were in the village. I, on the other hand, took the crest *à cheval*, astride, a foot dangling in space on either side, propelling myself forward with my hands in a crablike fashion. I felt a perfect fool in contrast to Benny, and judging from the Austrian snickers behind us, the girls seemed to agree! The last gendarme required a particularly delicate move: I had to face out and negotiate a corner, groping first for a hand-hold, then swinging my feet around. As I swung, my trousers caught on a nubbin of rock, and I was instantly separated from the seat of my pants. More Austrian laughter. Then, rappelling from the sharp point of the last gendarme, I missed the narrow platform and gashed a finger between the rope and the rock wall. Our return from Saas Grund to Stalden and then Zermatt resembled a military retreat. I was bandaged and bloodied and had tied my parka around my seat to cover my embarrassment.

Other trips were better. We made the first of a series of climbs with Benny's brother, Gottlieb, and his client—an American mother of five named Jane Horner. Jane and I got along right away, and it was pleasant to have congenial company on the climb. Our first trip together was the Roten Grat on the Alphubel—a six-hour climb over rock and—because of prevailing conditions that summer—snow and ice. The weather was ominous and the wind chilling. In one spot, Gottlieb was sweeping some snow from a ledge when his hand started to freeze. The long ridge gradually steepened as we approached the "big gendarme." But our progress was uninterrupted. On top, we barely paused before heading down over the easy Alphubel Glacier, glissading (skiing without skis) down some of the steeper slopes. This climb was one of my favorites, because it offered a thoroughly enjoyable combination—a challenging rock climb to the summit and then a swift and easy descent on snow. For those who may have the opportunity to climb in Zermatt, I highly recommend this route.

Incidentally, the Roten Grat offered an excellent illustration of the importance of having a guide on a climb of this nature. An English party—undoubtedly equally good or better climbers than myself—started off several days later without a guide. They had to spend the night in the open near the gendarme, and reaching the summit and then descending took them the whole next day. Alpine climbing involves a good deal more than just climbing. Route-finding holds the key to success on most of the big climbs. In fact, the standard routes on most of the mountains around Zermatt call for relatively limited tech-

A glissade

nical competence. Staying on the route is quite another matter!

The weather remained poor. A few days of sunshine were inevitably followed by a day or two of rain, with snow on the heights. The mountains never really had a chance to dry out. Nevertheless, we were able to ascend the Zinal Rothorn, one of Zermatt's best rock-climbing peaks. My panting decreased as I became used to the altitude.

In the midst of the foul weather, Benny, eager to do something, took me early one morning to Riffelalp by the Gornergrat train. We descended to the Gorner Glacier and then scrambled along the scree (loose rock) to the base of the Riffelhorn and a climb known as the Matterhorn Couloir. A couloir is a gully, generally five to twenty feet wide, which rises between walls of a mountain face. A gash in the rocks, this couloir rises for about a thousand feet inside the mountain and then finally opens out to a ledge from which rise the steep upper ridges of the miniature peak.

This trip marked the closest I've ever come to gymnastic climbing. There are many possible variations within the couloir, but Benny always seemed to choose the harder alternative. There were several overhangs—one nearly smooth wall—and several chasms to step over. Because of the lack of exposure, I was able to concentrate on the problems of the climb and truly enjoyed meeting and overcoming each pitch. Near the top of the couloir, the walls steepened and soared—nearly vertical—overhead. But the route went up the corner formed by the convergence of the two walls. Emerging from the gully, Benny was enthusiastic in his praise. For the first time I began to think that I might become a true climber rather than a mere bundle of firewood to be hauled up mountains by sturdy guides. We stepped out of the containing darkness

The Weisshorn

of the Matterhorn Couloir into the brilliant sunlight with the steep, exposed ridges rising over our heads. We fairly raced up the broken crests and were soon on top, three hours, more or less, from the glacier, a beautiful climb. We had some lunch and peacefully contemplated future climbs. Wherever Benny said I could go, I went.

One of the most exposed places in Zermatt is the Leiterspitzen, a jagged rock ridge above Täsch, with an elevation of about eleven thousand feet. Because of its relatively low altitude, it was free from snow and therefore climbable when higher peaks were not. Technically, the climb is stiffer than most in the Zermatt area, although it does not present the route-finding problems or the usual dangers of longer high-altitude climbs. Once again, we

climbed with Gottlieb and Jane. We took a taxi (the soft-
ness of the current generation!) to Täschalp, and at six
thirty in the morning we set out for the col,* a miserable
two-hour hike up loose scree.

From the col onward, the difficulties are considerable
and they begin immediately. The ridge bristled with gendarmes, each steeper and more exposed than the last.
Some pegs were already in place, but they made the
climbing possible rather than easy. The climbing was
nearly vertical; in places it was almost overhanging, yet,
surprisingly, I had no problems.

The exposure was enormous, with drops of several
thousand feet on either side of the ridge. In one place, the
crest actually had a hole in it. This spot—known as "the
window"—must be one of the airiest spots in the region.
Struggling up and down for nearly three hours, we over-
came each tower. One was so sharp that only one person
could sit astride it at the top. Finally the ridge ended, and
we wound up with a festive luncheon. Descending, the
four of us scrambled down a stony gully back to Täschalp
and consumed quarts of beer, lying on our backs in the
grass, looking up at the high peaks. A fantastic day!

The weather remained miserable. It was hard to believe that almost two months had gone by. It was now
August, and I had been living with Benny and his charm-
ing wife, Mathilde, in their villa, for the past month. We
tried to make big plans, but they were never carried out.
The endless pattern of alternating days of sunshine and
bad weather continued. I spent more and more hours in
Zermatt bars, where I met a delightful Danish boy, member of an extraordinary family. Peter Melchior and I became instant friends, and later I met his parents and two

---

* A col is the low point in a ridge, before it rises again, and is
generally the point of departure for a ridge climb.

younger sisters. The entire family has climbed the Matterhorn. Peter's father is now Danish ambassador to Switzerland, and all of his family share his love of the mountains.

One rainy day, Peter's sister, Anne, and I went with Benny and another Zermatt guide, Josef Petrig, to climb the cliffs that rise above the train station. There were only a few guides who would lead these vertical pitches, and my excitement was heightened by the fact that Benny had never been there before.

What followed was a bit of a circus. Our progress was followed from the village. People clustered around the telescope then in front of the Hotel Mont Cervin. Observers got their field glasses to see what we were doing. Above, we went doggedly up from ledge to ledge, the exposure extreme but the climbing quite straightforward. There was one key spot—the "crux." From this ledge it was necessary to traverse to the left, grope over an intervening ridge, find an elusive left handhold high above and over the ridge, and swing the left foot out into space and onto a convenient niche around the corner. I was frightened, but pride dictated silence and the pitch was overcome. There followed a tremendously exposed and upward-slanting traverse to the right that further froze my nerves. Finally, a grass ledge. The climb was over, and we could walk down!

Applause greeted us in the streets—it was an ego trip! But time was running out. These practice climbs were great fun, but Benny wanted to do one "big" climb before his pupil had to leave. With increasing regularity I heard the Sudwand on the Obergabelhorn mentioned. Whenever I asked, guides spoke with more than a healthy respect of the dark wall that towers several thousand feet above the Höhwang Glacier.

Soon enough, I was to learn that the wall deserved its reputation!

Chapter 3

The Sudwand
on the Obergabelhorn

The summer was nearing an end, Jane Horner and I had made a number of climbs together, looking toward a "big one." Peter Melchior, his mother, and his sister, Anne, had also made a number of climbs. We had hiked together, running down wherever possible to further strengthen our legs. Now the moment of decision was at hand.

Benny thought the 550-meter rocky Sudwand on the Obergabelhorn would "go," that is, could be climbed at that time. Others thought not, some being rather outspoken in their comments as to the insanity of the project. Technically, the climb rates on a scale with the Leiterspitzen, but is longer, higher, and—in the final vertical crack—more difficult. The face is seen to best advantage from Schwarzsee, where its beetling cliffs have to inspire respect.

We decided to make a party of ten—Peter and his mother and sister, Jane Horner and I, and the five guides—Benny, Gottlieb, Erwin Aufdenblatten, Josef Petrig, and Hieronymus (Rony) Inderbinen. We all knew one another, and it was a friendly if somewhat unwieldy group that agreed to meet at the church at midnight on August 24.

It was difficult to imagine what the next day would hold in store; we knew only that it would be a feat. Each of the five tourists prepared psychologically for the unknown. Anne and I elected to dance at the Broken Ski Bar until our departure, deciding that it would be impossible to get a meaningful amount of sleep before leaving. I danced the Charleston that night in climbing boots!

As the church clock tolled midnight, our group assembled. Soon after, we were threading our way by flashlight to the hamlet of Winkelmatten, and then through the woods and up steeply to Findelnbach Station. There, after a short delay, our "taxi"—a supply truck—transported us past Furi and Stafelalp and out to the moraine of the Höhwang Glacier, which lies beneath the fearsome wall.

It was hard to believe we were setting out on a major climb. There had been no hut walk, no watching the "Alpenglow," no restless sleep in the hut—in short, no assimilation into the world of the high mountains. And yet in the middle of the night we set foot on the glacial moraine, that loose deposit of stone and gravel which lies along the sides and ends of most glaciers.

At first it was easy, trudging up the moraine with the usual slipping and sliding. The snow was hard enough so that Gottlieb made a few nicks with his ice ax to facilitate our upward progress. We were still unroped. Speed was of the essence, particularly because of a rather large cornice that overhung the face at the summit. It was the sword of Damocles suspended over us. Several of the Zermatt guides had singled this out as the chief reason not to do the climb. Our guides were determined, but nevertheless respectful of the obvious dangers. The glacier was soon crossed and at the base of the cliff we all roped up.

The climbing immediately became interesting, but not overwhelming. The rock was steep, but it was broken up and there were plenty of good holds. We moved quickly, climbing together most of the time. Benny and Gottlieb stayed somewhat to the right of the Melchiors and their guides.

About halfway up the face, there was a difficult layback. This is a technique whereby a crack is climbed by placing one's toes on the far side of it and one's hands on the near side, using the opposing forces of one's arms and legs to balance upward. If it is difficult to describe, it is even more difficult to perform, at least it was for me.

Above this difficult crack, the face seemed to steepen appreciably. There were still plenty of holds, but the platforms were narrower and the resting places farther apart. The exposure was dizzying. My only concern was that we couldn't finish the climb and would have to scram-

The Zinal Rothorn with the Rothorn Ridge on the left

ble down those frighteningly steep cliffs. The climbing was the steepest I had ever attempted. Finally, we crawled around an intervening rib and onto a small platform. Above rose the crux, the long, slanting, smooth crack that would make or break the climb. There was an easier exit to the right, but to finish the climb correctly, the last crack must be taken head on. This was what Benny wanted to do, but there was a substantial problem: the entrance to the crack was filled with hard blue ice. To attempt to cut steps from such a precarious perch seemed impractical— in fact, impossible. Could we get over to the right-hand crack? The alternative did not appeal to Benny. With the enormous cornice threatening us some 150 feet above, Benny decided on a bold action plan. With no more than a "Wait here, Fred," he took off.

First he traversed left on a ledge not more than two inches wide. He worked his way over some ten to fifteen feet. Then from this nearly nonexistent stance, he utilized the layback technique to crawl up the thin crack that snaked up and to the right for about fifteen feet. The crack emptied into the main crack, just above the iced section.

I was awed by Benny's performance. I don't believe many men would have made that lead. When he was as secure as the airy crack permitted, he called to Erwin to join him. Using Benny's rope, Erwin quickly scrambled upward. When he, too, was "settled," they called me. I felt like a guinea pig, the first of the tourists to try a pitch that I knew, from watching, was harder than anything I had ever climbed. To be honest, I was scared stiff, dizzy from the exposure, and my confidence was sorely tested.

Somehow I made the "two-inch traverse," and was now under the layback pitch. Benny shouted at me to take Erwin's rope. But none of us had thought out the physics of this move. In the layback, my arms would pull me to the left, my feet would push me to the right. There was a pull from Benny's rope on the right that jarred my equilibrium somewhat. When I reached for Erwin's rope, the situation was as follows: my left hand was pulling me to the left, my legs were pushing me to the right, and the two ropes were pulling me to the right. The result was a traumatic half-minute I'll never forget. No sooner did I touch Erwin's rope than I lost my grip and pendulumed—right, left, right, left, and right once more. Suspended as I was over the void, space spun at my feet. I clutched at the holdless wall. On the fifth swing, I was able to stuff myself into a crack, my knees almost against my chest. My heart was pounding furiously, a result of what must have been the largest dose of adrenalin my body has ever produced. I was secure, if uncomfortable. The strain on Benny must have been enormous, but he never said a word other than: "Are you all right, Fred?" He and Erwin quickly decided it would be unwise to ask any of the other members to try the layback route. Instead, each would crawl up over me and the ice as best he or she could.

Shortly after my fall, a rock had detached itself from the face and made a target of Peter Melchior's head. Fortunately he had not been seriously hurt, although he had bled rather profusely. Indeed, our situation seemed desperate; the party was weakened and we were unsure of ourselves as we prepared to face the crux.

Somehow, the others got up that unfriendly cold crack. One by one, with appropriate grunts and heaves on the ropes, they moved upward. From first, I had fallen to last. When my name was finally called, an hour had passed and my legs were totally cramped. I stretched them as best I could and peered upward. As I looked down again, I was hit hard by a block of ice, which stunned me. I blacked out for an instant, came to quickly, and decided to get up as fast as possible.

But my muscles wouldn't respond. The slabs inside

Climbing in the Schawangunks

the crack were smooth, almost holdless. The distance between the fixed pitons, left there for future climbers' aid by an earlier party, was more than I could manage. I inched upward as best I could, and then rested my full weight on the rope. Benny held on, and Gottlieb helped. Those desperate moments are now fuzzy in my mind. Somehow I got up, alternately climbing and being held by Benny and Gottlieb as I marshaled my inner resources.

We had taken only four hours to climb the first sixteen hundred feet of the face. The last crack—about 100–150 feet—had cost us two hours! Our desperate adventure seemed successfully crowned. Jane Horner was so relieved to be on top that she threw herself down on the snow. Imagine her surprise and Gottlieb's concern when her seat proved to be the very lip of the cornice! It held, and Jane quickly moved back.

We descended the Arbengrat, the west ridge of the mountain. A good rock climb itself, it was a relief after the unrelenting verticality of the Sudwand. I climbed falteringly, physically and emotionally drained. The details of the descent escape me, other than an incident that occurred after we unroped. We were recrossing the moraine. It was about a foot wide—spacious after our climb—with a drop of several hundred feet on either side. As we trudged along, Anne Melchior suddenly tripped, lost her balance, and fell. Thanks to her good reflexes, she threw her arms over the top of the moraine, her feet dangling in space. As quickly as possible I dove on top of her. The incident was over in a matter of seconds, a near disaster that turned out to be nothing more than a good laugh, ilustrating the very thin line between comedy and tragedy.

Finally the moraine was passed and we picked up the Schönbiel path. The guides recoiled their ropes. Benny excused himself and left us. After the Sudwand, he was

off to the Täsch Hütte and a climb up the Teufelsgrat—
the Devil's Ridge—on the Täschhorn! This was a typical
combination for Benny—perhaps the strongest of the
Zermatt guides at this time.

Three days later I left Zermatt, depressed to think
that I probably would not return for many years. Now I
was setting out in the business world, and long climbing
vacations would have to wait until I had made my mark,
at which point I would probably be too old to truly enjoy
climbing.

Benny saw me off at the station. We had only a few
minutes, and there was so much I wanted to say. How
could I thank him for all he had done for me? How could
I express what the summer had meant to me? There was
no time. He helped me load my luggage, and the train
was moving. A quick handshake, "Thanks, Benny," and
he faded into the distance as the train rolled away from
Zermatt. I never had another opportunity to tell Benny
Perren what his friendship meant to me.

My parents met the freighter at the now defunct
Brooklyn Navy Yard. After recovering from their surprise
at seeing me fifty pounds lighter (it is hard to stay overweight if you climb!), the talk centered on Benny—his
ability, his friendliness, the way he inspired confidence.
My father had skied with him the previous winter and was
looking forward to a return engagement during the
coming season. We talked of the climbs I had made with
Benny, of other climbs Benny had made with other
clients. We talked of the Sudwand, of my father's days
skiing with Benny. We talked of Benny's home, where I
had lived; of his wife, Mathilde; of his child, expected in
October. In fact, we talked of Benny all the way home.

There was a letter waiting for me with a Zermatt
postmark. It was from Sylvia Coe, an American girl who

On the summit of the Matterhorn

had made many outstanding climbs with Benny. They had been planning to try the Sudwand together, and I thought the letter must contain the details of the climb. Before I even opened my bags to unpack, I ripped open the letter.

Dear Fred,
    I hate to have to write this letter, but Benny was killed last night . . .

My eyes filled with tears and it was with difficulty that I finished the letter. On August 31, Benny and Sylvia had set out about midnight for the Sudwand. Bad conditions—verglas * on the rocks—had forced them to turn

* A thin coating of ice.

back while they were still low on the face. Benny could never be idle, and had worked at home throughout the day. That evening he had loaded his supply truck and set out alone for the Grande Dixence hydroelectric project beyond Stafelalp. It was the last time he was seen alive.

In reconstructing the accident, it was evident that Benny's truck had hit a large stone in the road, flipped over, and plummeted down a gully next to the road. His neck was broken instantly. And so one of Zermatt's bravest men died in an automobile accident, just minutes from his native village, where automobiles were not permitted. It was grim irony. His funeral was one of the largest in the town's history—the entire Zermatt guide corps, all of the guides from Chamonix, the townspeople, Benny's countless skiing and climbing friends.

I cried myself to sleep that night, like a little child. My parents, with tears in their own eyes, could do little to comfort me. It was a sorrowful ending to what had been the happiest summer of my life.

In the fall, my working life began, in the syndicate department of Lehman Brothers, a Wall Street investment-banking firm. Certainly, extended Alpine tours had no place in my five-thousand-dollar salary. I served my apprenticeship happily, contenting myself with first weekly and then monthly slide shows to remind me of that summer, but I had no serious thoughts of climbing again in the near future. Then, in May, the head of the department, Andy Sage, suggested that I take a week's leave of absence and go to Switzerland for a three-week climbing holiday. The term "establishment" didn't exist in 1961, but it had never occurred to me that those in power would tolerate, let alone suggest extra time away from the office. I needed very little persuading, and in mid-July, I was back in my favorite mountain village.

There was some question as to whom I should climb with. I decided on Josef Petrig, whom I had introduced to Anne Melchior the previous summer and who had been with us on the Sudwand. He and I had drunk many beers together during the summer of 1960 and I liked him. It has always been important to me to regard my guide as a friend. Although there is always a professional guide/ client relationship, with very little effort it can develop into more. That summer, the weather was particularly bad. Our climbs were limited to a repeat of the climb over the train tracks, some special routes on the Riffel- horn, and a repeat of the Matterhorn Couloir. It was then that I realized I was more of a mountaineer than a pure rock climber. While the climbs we did were challenging —technically demanding—they lacked the special thrill of a high climb. Somehow, I felt somewhat cheated when it was time to go home.

But Josef and I had become good friends, and we knew we would have other summers to do the "big ones." Having had the opportunity to make this trip, I now vowed that I would climb every summer. And if other employers proved to be less understanding than Andy Sage, I planned to educate them to the benefits to be derived from Alpine holidays.

Several weeks after I returned home there was an- other letter from Zermatt, this time from Peter Melchior's father. Josef Petrig had fallen on the Obergabelhorn. He and his party had climbed the Sudwand and then, while descending the old route on the east face—in the company of two of his brothers, also guides—there had been an ac- cident. Josef and his client had fallen some fifteen hun- dred feet. Both were killed instantly.

Chapter 4

A New Beginning

The following summer business affairs prevented my returning to the Alps. I changed jobs, and in the interim it wasn't possible to get away. By 1963 I had lost what little nerve I had had for climbing. Nevertheless, I asked my employers for some extra time, and in July I was back in Zermatt, this time uncertain as to whether I would climb or simply hike.

My second day in Zermatt, I went up to the Hörnli Hut for a walk. Just as I arrived, Rony Inderbinen, another of the Sudwand group, appeared. We shook hands, chatted briefly, and arranged to meet in the village. Out of that meeting a partnership was formed that at this writing has lasted eleven years.

We made plans to go to the Rothorn Hut for a couple of days of climbing. First on the program was the Rothorn, an old friend, this time by the southwest ridge, the so-called Rothorngrat. It proved to be a beautiful climb over solid rock—one gendarme after another, nowhere very difficult, but continuously interesting. The ridge reminded me of a roller coaster. Rony and I moved well together and all too soon were at the summit. The return to the hut was over the "normal route," already familiar to me. Some soft snow in the couloir beneath the notch gave us a few anxious moments, but otherwise the descent was uneventful. It was only noon, and we spent most of the afternoon resting.

That evening Rony and I stood in front of the hut, watching the play of the Alpenglow on the high peaks and discussing the possibilities for the next day. The Wellenkuppe is what is commonly referred to as "an easy day for a lady." Actually, the mountain may be climbed directly from the Rothorn Hut by the normal route in about two and a half hours. Rony, clearly unhappy at the prospect of an uneventful slog up a lady's mountain, proposed that we add a little interest to the climb by setting out from the Triftjoch. He had never done the climb, nor had any of his contemporaries. Nevertheless, he had heard several of the old guides mention this route as being an extremely interesting one. From the Triftjoch, the ridge climbs about thirteen hundred feet to the summit of the Wellenkuppe. Unlike the solid spires of the Rothorn ridge which rise on the other side of the pass, the Wellenkuppe ridge offers a series of teetering and highly unstable rock piles, precariously perched between the Trift Glacier and the eastern extremity of the Mountet Glacier.

It was three thirty when we left the hut. The stars were twinkling, while the silhouettes of the mountains loomed black against the deep blue of the cloudless sky. We crossed the Trift Glacier and climbed the narrow tongue of ice and snow that leads one between the vertical rock walls to the Triftjoch, clearly visible from the Rothorn Hut. From here, Rony and I contemplated the first gendarme on the Wellenkuppe ridge.

Past experience in the mountains of the Valais—the canton in which I had done all my Alpine climbing—had led me to expect a rather easy start on a route that would gradually increase in difficulty. Indeed, it is one of the pleasant aspects of climbing in this region that one usually has several hours in which to wake up before the serious

The final tower on the Zinal Rothorn

difficulties must be tackled. The Wellenkuppe from the Triftjoch did not offer a transition period. No sooner had we climbed one rope length up the first gendarme than Rony came to an abrupt halt. He disappeared around the left side of the pinnacle, returned, probed to the right and even directly over the crest. Finally he traversed to the left, although the way was obviously difficult. I followed him out onto a thin slab, looped the rope around an outcropping rock, and waited as he edged his way around the corner. The rope barely moved, an ominous sign as I waited in the cold early morning light. More than an hour had passed and we had progressed no more than one hundred feet!

In twenty minutes I had payed out about fifteen feet of rope. Then Rony called me to follow. All I needed was one step around the corner to understand why he had been so slow. The gendarme met the ridge at right angles, with an overhang effectively blocking the point at which the ridge was to be regained. It was necessary to traverse several steps to the left, step onto a hip-high sloping foothold, place all the weight on that minute outcropping, and then somehow pull up onto the knife-edge crest. Above, Rony looked none too comfortable standing in two tiny nicks in the crest itself with the rope belayed around a small nubbin of rock above him.

I set out cautiously, working my way up the corner. It was delicate work, since the only holds were on rotten rocks projecting from the corner. I expected each and every handhold and foothold to come away, with me attached. As I prepared for the short traverse that proved to be the crux of the climb, Rony informed me that he was getting tired and that I had better move a little more quickly. One look at him convinced me of the urgency of his request. I was at the top of the corner; now, two steps to the left, and then—I was off! In my anxiety to reach up for the narrow crest above, I had failed to keep my left foot pressed against the nubbin of rock supporting me.

Time is a very relative measure. Actually, I wasn't detached from the rock for more than a few seconds, yet it seemed a desperate and prolonged crisis. The tiny nubbin of rock around which the rope was belayed withstood the strain. The pull on Rony's rope had come from above, rather than from below, in which case he would scarcely have been able to hold me. Reacting to the immediate danger, I somehow hurriedly swarmed up the seemingly holdless rock and grabbed onto the bucket holds of the ridge. My right hand was covered with blood, but, fortunately, as we cleaned it up, we saw that the wounds were all superficial. No sooner were the bandages secured than Rony turned his gaze once more to the summit, still twelve hundred feet above us. If Rony had misgivings, they were never reflected in his expression.

We continued on. The next section of the ridge consisted of a twenty-foot quasi-hand traverse.* There were small outcroppings of rock on which we placed the tips of our boots as we swung along on our hands. The rock continued to be excessively loose, and we inched our way along the crest, trying to find the most solid rock. We gradually began to gain height, although our progress was slow and very cautious along the length of the ridge. Far below, we could see a group of climbers returning from the Wellenkuppe by the regular route. Our goal, the gentle snowcap that leads to the summit of the Wellenkuppe, was still quite distant. I began to get discouraged about the outcome of our adventure.

It was now eight o'clock. We had been climbing virtually without a rest for four and a half hours. We topped another pinnacle, and I heard Rony complain that

---

* A hand traverse is a pitch on which there are no proper footholds, therefore necessitating one's full weight being held by the hands.

perhaps these towers would go on forever. But the worst was behind us. A half hour of step cutting in ice, a few more pinnacles, and we had reached the summit ridge. At nine thirty, after six hours of climbing, continuously exposed since we had left the Triftjoch, we stood on the crest of our "lady's peak." We settled back for a leisurely survey of the surrounding peaks.

It was close to ten thirty when we quit the summit, and by noon we were trudging up the last boulders to the hut. It had been a rather active "rest" day following our traverse of the Rothorn ridge, and it was amusing to listen to Hans Furrer, the hut guardian, describe our slow progress, which he had witnessed through his field glasses. Indeed, our lady's mountain had held out several surprises. It was a climb we both look back on with special satisfaction.

Later that week, we climbed the Rimpfischhorn, one of the peaks between Zermatt and Saas Fee, from the Fluhalp. We had intended to traverse the rocky north ridge, but when we arrived on the summit five hours after setting out, I ran out of energy. Over the years, I have found that three climbs in a week are too much for me. This was my first proof. The moment we started down, I felt better, and we virtually ran over the rocks and then snow, passing everyone on the way back to the Fluhalp.

The summer of 1963 was important to me for two reasons. It was the first time I had climbed over four thousand meters since my fall on the Obergabelhorn in 1960, and I discovered that what little nerve I had possessed was still there. Second, I discovered a true friend— a sympathetic climbing partner—in Rony Inderbinen. There were many peaks, many adventures in store for Rony and me.

Chapter 5

Earthbound Ego

While these relatively heroic ascents were being accomplished, my self-image as a climber remained abysmally low. A day's outing—just an hour and a half from New York—proved that while my mountaineering abilities had improved and my experience had broadened, I was not about to threaten the supermen.

The Schawangunks lie due west of New Paltz, just across the river from Poughkeepsie, New York. Boyd Everett, later to die in an ice avalanche on Dhaulagiri, one of the world's highest peaks, persuaded me to try a day of rock climbing on these nearby cliffs. I denigrated the idea, but finally condescended to join Boyd and some of his friends in what I felt was an obvious comedown for a Matterhorn man. On the way up to the "Gunks," I regaled the troops with immodest accounts of the Matterhorn. Memory had kindly blurred the less fortunate details of the climb. Pounding heart, burning lungs, splitting headache—all were forgotten. So, too, were the horrors of the descent, whose focal point had been my rear!

Once we sighted the cliffs, my monopoly of the conversation ceased. They were steep. Yes, I was told, they *do* overhang. I was told, too, that climbs ranged from 5.1 to 5.10. I didn't have the nerve to admit that I had no

Al Zesiger climbing on Mount Mansfield

idea what the numbers meant. I did know that this was
an entirely new world to me, a world that looked far more
difficult than the Matterhorn. The equipment was new to
me too—bongs, rurps, angles (new types of mountain
hardware, special sizes of pitons and wedges), and climbing shoes that looked more like sneakers than the high-
backed boots with which I was familiar. Helmets were in
evidence, and complicated belays were common practice.

One climb, and my bluff was called. We did something called the Easy V. The V stood for a German word
that referred to the crux where the head was used to overcome a steep chimney. The "Easy" was a gross misrepre-
sentation as far as I was concerned.

The first pitch was reasonable, relatively speaking,

although it was harder than anything I had done on the Matterhorn. The ledge at the top of the pitch was only about a foot and a half wide. Since I was the weakest of the three climbers, I was in the middle. This meant that once I got to that narrow ledge, I had to belay the leader as he climbed the next pitch, and then secure the last man up the first pitch. This proved to be too long a stay at my exposed aerie.

There was no second pitch for me. Suffering from the exposure, I became increasingly afraid of the first move on the next pitch. It involved stepping off the belay ledge onto a thin hold about two feet to the left and then proceeding up a steep, rocky gully. My ego in ashes, I announced that I would not be able to climb it. When asked why, I admitted that it was nothing physical; rather, it was fear. Boyd calmly talked to me for about a half an hour, restating his confidence in my ability to do the climb. Finally, he saw the hopelessness of his mission, and a rappel was prepared. Ignominiously, I roped down the sixty feet, utterly shattered.

On the ground once more, I resolved never to go near a rock again. An hour later, after a masterful sales job by Boyd, I was roped up and ready to attack another climb, this one with the seemingly self-contradictory name of the Easy Overhang. Here again, there was verticality. However, the ledges were wider and the holds more obvious. Somehow I got up, pleased to have made a climb, but still far from overconfident!

Over the years, I have returned to the Gunks a number of times, but there is no doubt that I am not a rock climber. Mountaineers generally look for the path of least resistance up a mountain. Naturally, the more advanced climbers seek harder routes with greater challenges, but nevertheless the path of least resistance is the general rule. Mountaineering requires endurance, self-discipline,

and a head for heights. However, gymnastic ability is not
a prerequisite. In fact, average coordination is more than
enough. Rock climbing is another story altogether. Here,
extreme balance, superior coordination, and acrobatic
skills are necessary. Rock climbers look for the paths of
most resistance. Climbs are measured numerically (5.1
being the easiest and 5.10 being the hardest), the grading
based on the relative difficulty of the hardest moves on
the routes. Longer climbs also are given Roman numeral
ratings from I to VI (VI being the most difficult), depend-
ing on how sustained the difficulties are.

In mountaineering, motion is usually continuous,
both climbers moving together on all but the most difficult pitches. In rock climbing, climbers rarely move
together; progress is made one at a time, one climber belaying and protecting the other. This is known as technical
climbing. When the climbers cannot progress on their
own, aids such as pitons (wedges), carabiners (clips),
and ladders and ropes are used to move upward. This is
"artificial" climbing.

I have done no artificial climbing and have attempted
technical climbing of only a middle degree of difficulty.
Frankly, I don't enjoy the Schawangunks. I like to climb
rocks on the way to the summit of a high peak, but I don't
enjoy rock climbing for the sake of rock climbing. You
don't need to be a rock specialist to enjoy the Alps or
many of our Western peaks, or even to climb the Hima-
layas! Having proved my shortcomings on rock, my enthusiasm for the mountains remained as strong as ever.

In the summer of 1964, I led my first Alpine climb,
with Bernard Roth of Strasbourg, France, and Susan Gil-
lespie of Rye, New York. The Breithorn is the easiest four-
thousand-meter peak in the Zermatt area, but it is still a
long and high climb. It was an undeniable thrill to be
first on the rope, a new dimension of adventure. We set

out from Schwarzsee to cross the Theodul Glacier to Testa Grigia, at an altitude of 3500 meters. The signpost said four hours; under my expert leadership, we arrived at our destination in just under seven.

The absence of a guide was noticeable immediately. The rope got snarled several times. I unerringly guided us to the edge of every crevasse on the glacier. Steps were laboriously chopped when an easy route lay several feet away had I but seen it. I would never have passed the guide school exam, but we did get to Testa Grigia. My friends were sympathetic. My embarrassment was heightened by their kindness; not a word was spoken on the subject of my leadership. The next morning we reached the summit in two and a half hours, thanks to the beaten track from which even I couldn't stray.

It was a great moment: I was back on top of the world I had shared with Benny just four years earlier. There was also the undeniable thrill of having gotten there on our own, and for me, the satisfaction of giving pleasure to my friends. Their faces were radiant as we drank in the 360-degree panorama the Breithorn offers on a clear day. We spent almost an hour on top and then decided to prolong the adventure by traversing the Klein Matterhorn on the way down.

Although I had not climbed the peak, I had heard from the guides that, despite its rocky appearance from the Zermatt side, it was primarily a snow climb with a little rock scrambling from the southern approach. With exaggerated caution, I guided our little group over the easy rock pitches. It wasn't really climbing, but at the high altitude (nearly thirteen thousand feet), one couldn't be too careful. On the summit, we were greeted by an icy blast of wind from the north and descended immediately.

Down near Testa Grigia, the north wind brought a

heavy snowstorm. We marched down the glacier to the Gandegg Hut, having decided it would be unwise to risk recrossing to Schwarzsee, since it would probably take even more than seven hours with zero visibility!

There is no doubt that given the ability, training, and courage, the best way to enjoy the mountains is with friends. If you can develop a friendship with a guide, it offers an acceptable, if expensive, alternative.

Two more experiences that summer broadened my climbing horizons. The first was a high-level traverse of Monte Rosa. The mountain has eleven summits over four thousand meters; Rony and I decided to climb five of them in a day. Once the altitude has been gained, the peaks can be climbed consecutively by traversing snow

Fred Jacobson near the shoulder of the Matterhorn

Benny Perren on the summit of the Riffelhorn with the
Matterhorn in the background

and rock ridges. Within the second hour of what was to be a fifteen-hour day, I found myself looking up at the sky through the lips of a crevasse! The Grenz Glacier is notorious for its crevasses, and it took me no time at all to find one to my liking. Rony pulled me out with the help of Artur Sigrist, another Zermatt guide. In the twenty minutes I spent dangling at the end of the rope, I had a chance to observe how easy it would be to have a one-way trip to the depths. The crevasse widened, blue ice walls on either side. My fingers, pinned between the rope and the ice, quickly froze. Once liberated from the icy crypt, they hurt terribly as they thawed out. I could only imagine the pain suffered by climbers whose extremities have been frozen for days!

After this unpromising start, all went well. We climbed the glacier and reached the summit of the Signalkuppe. On top, the Capanna Margherita is perched—the highest hut in Europe, at almost fifteen thousand feet. From here we climbed the Zumsteinspitze, the Ostspitze, the Grenzgipfel, and finally the Dufour, the highest point in Switzerland. This time, there was no labored breathing —it was like walking in Vermont, only over rock and snow rather than dirt trails. On the Dufour, it was so still that Rony could light his pipe with a single match! This was my longest climb, yet it was enjoyable from start to finish. Climbing certainly needn't be a masochistic ordeal.

The other broadening experience in 1964 was less positive. Rony and I decided to traverse the Nadelgrat, a series of four-thousand-meter peaks linked by rock and snow ridges. The climb is done from the Dom Hut, and the guidebook describes the walk to the hut as "a notable slog." The hut is located at the edge of the Festi Glasier, 5500 feet above Randa, the point of departure, and is fully exposed to the afternoon sun. We climbed up quickly, rather too quickly. Overheated and thirsty, I ordered a quart of the local apple juice and chugalugged with gusto. That evening as I lay in my bunk my stomach gave the first indications that I had made a terrible mistake. By morning, the damage was complete. With unwavering courage, I declared that we would make the climb anyway. After three hours of staggering drunkenly between the crevasses—and with our sought-after ridge in sight—we decided mutually to call off the attempt. By that evening, my stomach was fine, but the climb had been lost. I have never had apple juice at a hut since.

Chapter 6

New Peaks

In 1965, Rony and I added a few more peaks to our "bag." The Strahlhorn was climbed from Fluhalp on my twenty-seventh birthday. The highlights of the climb included our being lost for an hour on the moraine, my stepping into three or four concealed crevasses, and a spell of breathlessness such as I have never experienced before or since in the mountains.

Later on we returned to the Weissmies Hut above Saas Grund, scene of my shame with the Austrian girl. This time we traversed two four-thousand-meter peaks—the Fletschhorn and the Lagginhorn—and stayed at the hut an extra night to climb the Weissmies. Coming down from the Lagginhorn, we had an unparalleled view of the Mischabel range, and I decided that someday I would *have* to revisit the Nadelgrat as well as the Dom and the Täschhorn. It was during this trip to Saas Fee that I first had the idea of trying to climb all the major peaks in the Zermatt area—the thirty-seven "four-thousanders."

The summer of 1966 saw us back at our task. With beautiful September weather, we climbed the Pointe de Zinal and then traversed the Allalinhorn from the Täsch Hut over the Fee Kopf and down to Saas Fee. From Saas Fee, we climbed to the Almagelleralp, our plan being to do the Portjengrat the following day. This is a well-known rock climb, which we hoped would be good training for bigger projects.

We stayed at the Almagelleralp Hotel the night before our climb. It was tended by an extremely shy, plain girl who thought we were interested in her (perhaps she'd heard of my Weissmies Hut caper with the Austrian girl!). Only after repeated assurances that we were there to climb mountains did she agree to show us the sleeping quarters. Would we like sheets on our bed? Of course— a rare luxury in mountain inns. We changed our minds when the gray-black sheets were folded back. Thank you, but just plain mattresses and blankets would be more than satisfactory. We were led from the deluxe quarters to the

View from the heights above Saas Fee

plain world of blankets only. I sat on the bed, and Rony was immediately obscured by a dense cloud of dust. Without a doubt, this was the filthiest hovel either of us had ever seen. It was hard to believe that we were in Switzerland. We debated sleeping outside, but decided against this Spartan alternative. This was a mistake, however, for during the night, I suffered my first attack of asthma in six years, undoubtedly triggered by the dust-laden atmosphere. The next morning we stretched the three-hour hike to the ridge into four hours. At the base of the rocks, where the interesting climbing begins, I ran out of breath. Today, the "Almageller Hilton" is under new and more typically Swiss management!

Our program was thrown back by this failure, but

Summit cornice on the Weissmies

there was still time for one big climb. In 1964, we had climbed five of the eleven peaks on the Monte Rosa. Now we wanted to do five more, the so-called little peaks, each of them over thirteen thousand feet. A logistical problem arose, however. Rony had another client in Zermatt who was equally anxious to climb. He had waited the previous week while Rony and I had climbed some twenty thousand feet together. Now he had his heart set on the Signalkuppe on Monte Rosa. Herr N. wished to spend the night at the Margherita Hut, in order to enjoy the sunrise from three miles above sea level.

Herr N. did not have the ideal build for mountaineering; he was six foot seven and weighed about 270 pounds. His weight was unfortunately concentrated about his middle. All in all, he was not an ideal second on a heavily crevassed glacier, which the Grenz Glacier was. Through its ice fall lay the route to the Signalkuppe and the Margherita Hut. Rony would not think of going alone with the ponderous Herr Doktor on the glacier. Instead, he proposed to take him around to Italy by car or train and climb the Signalkuppe from the Gnifetti Hut. Not only is the route far easier and less dangerous, but the Gnifetti Hut is also some 2500 feet higher than the Monte Rosa Hut, making for a much shorter day.

This was an ideal solution, save for one fact. I was scheduled to visit with friends in Bergamo and had to leave Zermatt on Friday. Rony would not get back to Zermatt until late Tuesday night or Wednesday afternoon. We would have to go to a hut Wednesday evening and make the climb and return to Zermatt on Thursday. My bags would have to be packed for the eight thirty train Friday morning. And, if the weather were doubtful on Wednesday or Thursday, I would lose my opportunity for the "big" climb to cap off the season. Rony and I had

climbed together for four seasons, and we were both unhappy with that plan, so a compromise was promptly
devised. I would accompany Rony in escorting Herr
Doktor over the Grenz and up to the snowfields of the
Lysjoch. From there, we would climb the five "little"
peaks of the Monte Rosa—the Parrotspitze, Ludwigshöhe,
Schwarzhorn, Balmenhorn, and Vincents Pyramide. Herr
Doktor would join us on as many of these peaks as he
liked. If he should be tired, we could easily unrope from
him, leaving him to rest at the various cols. When the five
had been climbed, we would then head back to the Signalkuppe and a night at the Margherita Hut.

Herr Doktor liked the plan. It would enable him to
ascend a glacier where he could not ordinarily have been
taken. And, too, there would be someone to share the
fee—not inconsiderable for this long a climb. I liked the
plan because it assured me of the big climb I was after.
If we succeeded, only the Nordend would remain for me
to climb in the Monte Rosa massif. We met at the Gorner-
gratbahn on Sunday afternoon, September 11. I had my
first doubts when I noted that Herr Doktor either possessed no ice ax or didn't think the Grenz would require
one. I said nothing. He spoke no English, and my German
was easy to misunderstand.

The three of us descended from the train at Rotenboden, where signs pointed the way to the hut across the
Gorner Glacier. It is one of the most pleasant, least fatigu-
ing hut walks around Zermatt. Markers guide one safely
across the glacier, and the hut is only about two hours
of easy walking from the railroad station. As the sun
started to sink behind the Matterhorn, the lower Gorner
Glacier was wrapped in shadow. Higher up, the snows of
the Cima di Jazzi and the Fillarhorn were bathed in deep
yellow. Behind us, the Riffelhorn towered above the

glacier, looking more like an inaccessible pinnacle than the practice peak that it is. Not a cloud in the sky—it was good to be alive!

Since it was already the middle of September, the hut was not too crowded. We slept soundly from eight until we were awakend at three; we stumbled out into the night. While countless stars glittered overhead, the new moon was no help in lighting our way. It was four o'clock as we trained our lanterns on the moraine ahead of us. Lanterns twinkled above us on the glacier and voices carried mysteriously across the expanse ahead. The black silhouette of the Matterhorn towered in the distance to the west. Immediately to our right, the Lyskamm's tremendous bulk seemed to glow in the dark.

A good hour's scrambling ensued, complete with the usual swearing, cries of anguish, slippery footing, barked shins—a typical moraine. The sky was lightening as we roped ourselves together and stepped out onto the Grenz Glacier, leaving the usual route to the Dufourspitze behind us on our left. We set out at a slow pace. The lower portion of the Grenz Glacier usually offers few problems, despite my earlier fall into one of its crevasses. Crevasses are generally well marked, with solid bridges leading over them. Higher up, however, it is more broken as one approaches the Lysjoch and the Italian frontier. This summer, the upper section was unusually broken up, and we were forced to take a different route, far to the left.

It wasn't long before we came to a rather sizable crevasse that couldn't be bypassed. Its upper lip rose vertically for perhaps ten or fifteen feet. As Rony explored the length of the crack, fragments of German sentences escaped from Herr Doktor. "My arms are weak." "It doesn't go." "This is too much." And, as I approached: "Help me with my crampons!" The poor fellow was used to the "tilted tennis courts" of the Breithorn and the

Rimpfischhorn. Indeed, he seemed to sense the depths of the crevasse reaching up for him. We waited while Rony searched out a point of weakness. Meanwhile, I put on my companion's crampons for him. My hands, frostbitten on this very glacier just two years before, told me that it was freezing cold. Perched on a forty-five-degree slope, we waited and shivered.

Finally, the call to follow floated down from above. With considerable difficulty, we bridged the chasm and heaved ourselves up on the other side. Ahead of us, the angle of the slope increased to almost fifty degrees for several hundred feet. It was solid shiny ice! Rony chopped up about sixty feet, carved out a platform in the ice, and called to the Doktor to follow. I gave him my ice ax, hoping to increase his confidence. I have never felt more helpless! The large man was slipping about in the steps Rony had cut. Had he fallen we would never have been able to support the inevitable strain. But he persevered, and an hour and a half later, we were over the crux. It had seemed like a full day's work. The shorter portion of the rope was between the Doktor and me, and most of the time I was unbelayed! The memory of that ice slope still lingers ominously.

As we plodded up the snowfields immediately below and to the left of the Lysjoch, Herr Doktor faded. Then an Italian party, on their descent after climbing up from Italy, informed us that the Margherita Hut was closing that day. A change in plans was necessary, and we were already two hours behind schedule, thanks in part to the difficulties of the ice wall and in part to the fact that above the wall the German needed to stop every five minutes to regain his breath. It was eleven o'clock. Now, for the first time, Herr Doktor informed us of his intention to add the Zumsteinspitze to his bag of peaks. Since this was in the opposite direction from the "little" peaks, and since I

had already climbed it as well as the Signalkuppe, I was
not particularly keen for the plan. But while the Doktor's
imagination expanded, his upward mobility tailed off
sharply. In fact, soon he was no longer capable of any
upward motion whatsoever. We left him sitting in the
snow under solemn oath that he would not move while
we were gone. Once on our own, Rony and I picked up
the pace. In fact, we almost ran—no mean feat at just
under fifteen thousand feet! Rony proposed that he and I
climb four of the five little peaks as quickly as possible.
Rony would then go back for Herr Doktor, take him up
something if he was able, and return to the Balmenhorn
Hut, where I was to wait for him. Then we would all
descend to the Gnifetti Hut, where we would spend the
night.

We first did the Parrotspitze. A narrow and airy,
though easy, ridge led to the summit. It was an exquisite
tightrope: to our left, the giants of the Valais and the
Oberland spread out before us; to the right, the clouds
boiled up the twelve-thousand-foot east face of the Monte
Rosa. The Cresta del Soldato—the Soldier's Ridge—seemed
to rise out of bottomless depths. There was a tremendous
wind on top, so we turned without delay and hurried
down the ridge. From the Piodejoch, we quickly mounted
the easy slopes of the Ludwigshöhe and in short order
stood on our second summit. Another handshake, and
down again, this time to the Zurbriggenjoch, from which
we headed for the steep face of the Schwarzhorn.

Truly a "continental miniature," the Schwarzhorn
nevertheless presents an excessively steep 150-foot snow
slope in excess of fifty degrees. By now we were moving
as one, and before long we were seated on the summit
rocks. It was a glorious day, and the sun warmed us with
the joy of life in the high mountains.

We then crossed the Lys Glacier to scramble up the

Balmenhorn. There is a small cabin on its summit maintained by the Italian Alpine Club, just below the larger-than-life statue of Christ looking out over Italy. I was to wait there while Rony took Herr Doktor for some climbing. It was only two o'clock; we had climbed the four peaks in less than three hours.

Left alone, I sat gazing at the magnificent surroundings. My meditations were interrupted by two members of the Arona section of the Italian Alpine Club whose heavy duty it was to lead a rescue party in retrieving the bodies of two fallen comrades. With the brilliant blue sky and warm sun smiling down on us, it was hard to comprehend death—a grim reminder of the price mountains extort for mistakes.

Vincents Pyramide taken from inside the Balmenhorn Hut with the Cresta del Soldato on the left

After what seemed like half a day (it was actually four hours), Rony returned with a rejuvenated Herr Doktor. They had climbed the much desired Signalkuppe, and added the Zumsteinspitze for good measure. The German, getting his second wind, had realized his ambition. And Rony had set a new standard for perseverance—six peaks in one day! However, Rony didn't consider his peak-bagging performance finished. As I was admiring the oncoming sunset, Rony pointed out that it would be "uninteresting" to have to come back another time to do the Vincents Pyramide. We had better than an hour of daylight remaining and flashlights to boot!

Our ascent of the Vincents was pure comedy. Herr Doktor had an immediate relapse and was now completely spent. Barely able to move, he nevertheless insisted that he should accompany Rony and me on at least one peak. Rony went first and I was in the middle, insulating Rony from our friend who brought up the rear. He also brought us up—at almost every step. He would stop in his tracks, pull me backward, and I in turn would drag on Rony. But he wouldn't hear of unroping. Finally, at seven ten, the three of us stood on the summit. It was a strange feeling to stand on a fourteen-thousand-foot peak at such a late hour. The dark clouds bathed the black silhouettes of the brooding peaks, and the stillness enveloped us. We were at peace with ourselves and our beloved mountains.

As we descended to the Gnifetti Hut, darkness fell rapidly. I was leading down, while Rony protected us from the rear. Farther on, Rony and I switched positions so that he might lead through the crevasses that line the route to the hut. My light burned out, and the doctor's huge bulk effectively blocked the light from his lamp. An electrical storm was boiling up from the south, and as I stumbled along in the dark, I began to fear that perhaps we had overextended ourselves. It got darker and darker;

the lightning moved closer. The morale of our little group plummeted. When we finally stumbled on the hut, it was eight thirty, and in our state of fatigue, it took us ten minutes to figure out where the door to the Gnifetti Hut was located!

Once inside, I had a chance to employ my newly acquired Italian. Yes, we could have some bread and soup. Rony, an even-tempered, almost saintly man, let out a sudden oath. Hoping to find a few extra morsels of food in his rucksack, he discovered that the inside was covered with jam! He had left the sack with Herr Doktor, so that the two of us might move faster. Wishing to spare his own sack, Herr Doktor had used Rony's as a seat to shield him from the snow. When 270 pounds of flesh meet a couple of ounces of jam, the results can easily be imagined!

Rony and I agreed that it would be unwise to descend the Grenz with Herr Doktor. So, all of the next day was spent in descending to Alagna, Italy, and getting back to Zermatt. We were delayed on an easy snowfield because the doctor insisted on roping up; we missed the cable car to Alagna because of an hour's time difference between Italy and Switzerland. In pouring rain, we spent most of the rest of the day in cars, taxis, and finally a cable car from Cervinia at the foot of the Italian ridge of the Matterhorn to Testa Grigia, overlooking the Theodul Pass. From there, we descended the Theodul Glacier, arriving back in Zermatt at dusk.

Another summer gone. The mountains had favored us. And yet, the Nordend remained. So, too, did the Lyskamm. And the Mischabel peaks and the glorious Dent Blanche. My Alpine appetite—rather than being satisfied—was growing.

Chapter 7

The Dent Blanche

As a regular visitor to the Swiss Valais, I had long been intrigued by the jagged ridges and crenellated faces of the Dent Blanche. Technically, it was rated one of the harder "regular" routes around Zermatt, and it wasn't climbed often. In my "armchair" years, I had read a great deal about the peak, and recollections of these tales further piqued my interest.

The mountain was first climbed in 1862 by one of the famous pioneers, Thomas S. Kennedy, and a Mr. Wigram, in the company of Jean-Baptiste Croz and one of the Kronigs from Zermatt. Just six days before the actual conquest, Kennedy had attempted the peak with the Peter Taugwalders, father and son. These two were to win enduring fame as the first conquerers of the Matterhorn just three years later. On the Dent Blanche, however, the older Taugwalder, who was leading, slipped and almost fell on the steep, slippery rocks. The mishap so unnerved him that Kennedy was forced to take the lead himself, but even then Taugwalder found himself too shaken to follow. Greatly disappointed, Kennedy returned to Zermatt. A few days later, with new guides, he stood on the summit of the proud peak. His description of the first climb is striking:

Great castles of shattered rock sprang directly out
of the ridge . . . a slip might have endangered the
lives of the whole party . . . giddy work for unaccustomed hands. The rocky towers above us were
broken into wildly fantastic groups.

That was in 1862. Today, with the benefit of one
hundred years of climbing experience, the mountain by
its south ridge (the normal route) is described differently
in modern guidebooks:

It is preferable to turn the Grand Gendarme on the
left by the West face. Then follow the crest, more or
less, to the summit. The second gendarme is generally
turned on the right (East) near its summit, by a ledge
and an easy chimney (large blocks); the third, to
the left (West) by slabs, which are often iced and
difficult, under a vertical wall which is climbed by
a crack . . .

While the guidebook points out that the route is
"subject to high mountain hazards—rapidly deteriorates
on the advent of a storm," it nevertheless summarizes
the climb as "quite straightforward in good conditions."
Need we ever doubt that familiarity breeds contempt?

In any event, Thursday, August 31, 1967, found three
of us at the little hamlet of Furi boarding a truck that
would take us up the Zmutt valley as far as Hohwang,
an hour or two below the Schönbühl Hut. Rony and I
were joined by Norbert Kaltenkirchen, a young bakery
owner from Gelsenkirchen, Germany, another of Rony's
clients. It was the beginning of an enduring friendship,
and Norbert and I have climbed together regularly since
then.

I had arrived in Zermatt less than a week earlier.
My first day was spent practicing with Rony on the

Riffelhorn. The following day we had traveled by train to Sierre—in the Rhône Valley—and from there by a hair-raising bus ride to Zinal at the head of the Val d'Anniviers. We had hiked up some five thousand feet to the Cabane Tracuit, from which we had climbed the Bieshorn—our first four-thousand-meter peak of the summer. On returning to Zermatt, we discovered that Norbert had arrived and was ready to go. After a brief meeting, the Dent Blanche was agreed upon as our target. Norbert was an expert rock climber, so Rony didn't mind taking us both on the same rope, rather an unusual practice on this major climb, where climbers must move one at a time over many of the more difficult pitches, and speed is therefore of the essence.

It snowed on Wednesday, and Norbert and I were somewhat reluctant to set out directly the next day, since the Dent Blanche has the reputation of being particularly difficult when it is iced up. Other guides warned against leaving so soon after the snow. Norbert and I, fearing verglas, suggested sleeping at Schönbühl on Thursday, climbing the Tête Blanche and the Tête de Valpelline Friday, and sleeping at the Rossier Hut before setting out for the Dent Blanche on Saturday. This would give the mountain an extra day to dry, and, besides, the Rossier Hut was situated at 3500 meters, some three thousand feet above the Schönbühl. This would shorten the expedition by two to three hours and make the actual climbing more enjoyable, since we would be fresh when we arrived at the foot of the ridge proper.

Rony liked the second part of the suggestion and agreed that we should sleep at Rossier. However, he was eager to climb the Dent Blanche without delay, since he feared a possible change in the weather. While I am strong-willed in many ways, I had long since stopped second-guessing mountain guides in the mountains! Therefore, at eleven o'clock Thursday morning, Norbert and I met Rony and proceeded to the cable car that would transport us to Furi, where our "taxi" awaited us. Much to Rony's chagrin, our truck and driver weren't on schedule. So Norbert and I used the half hour to good advantage, dining on soup, sausage, eggs, *rösti*, and bread. Later events were to prove this delay—annoying at the time—most providential.

Before long, our transport materialized, and by one o'clock we were at Höhwang, starting the trudge up to the Schönbühl. It was a beautiful day, and the three of us were joyous. After pausing briefly for refreshments at the Schönbühl, we promptly set out for our first objective—the Rossier Hut, known also as the Cabane de la Dent Blanche.

Our path led up the steep and dusty moraines of the Schönbühl Glacier. In a short time, we reached the glacier itself, where we roped up for the crossing to the Wandfluh. We were more than a little disconcerted to note that the weather was rapidly deteriorating. Dully, we plodded across the glacier and up a steep snow gully to the start of the Wandfluh. The Wandfluh is a wall of rock, about two thousand feet high, which connects the south ridge of the Dent Blanche with the Col d'Hérens and the Tête Blanche. It seems a sheer precipice when viewed from a distance. On closer inspection, it proved to be a ruinous slag heap. Solid hand- and footholds were nonexistent as we scrambled upward, fearing every moment that the loose stones—with ourselves attached—should be propelled down the mountainside to the glacier. It seemed endless. However, as with all unpleasant passages, the Wandfluh was eventually beneath us as we crossed the névés * forming the lower section of our ridge. Our height was

---

* Upper Alpine snowfields.

over twelve thousand feet, and it was necessary to descend some six hundred feet to the Rossier. After a prolonged halt for tea, photography, route-finding, scenery appreciation, and general camaraderie, we headed due west.

Our gentle snowfield suddenly turned into a rather sharp snow ridge. All at once Norbert, who was in the lead, started slipping around. Rony cried out a warning to stay in the steps; it was very dangerous footing.

A few more steps forward and the three of us found ourselves clambering onto an ice ridge. We hewed out little platforms for ourselves, making good use of our ice axes. Once our stances were improved, we put on our crampons and inched cautiously down the miniature ridge. A short but steep rock passage followed, and we were at the hut. We were surprised when we looked at our watches—ten after seven!

It didn't matter—we would order a hearty supper and still be in bed by eight thirty. However, to our keen disappointment, we learned that the guardian of the hut had that day descended to Ferpècle. No hotel service! This meant boiling one's own water, doing one's own cooking and washing up, and—most important—providing one's own food. Rony thought sadly of the lunch at Furi that he hadn't shared. Norbert and I speculated on the value of having a half-starved guide to lead us up the Dent Blanche. We threw ourselves on the kindness of fellow climbers in the hut—a sort of high-altitude Salvation Army act. Thanks to their generosity, our ravenous trio feasted on tea without sugar, stale bread, a little dried meat, and a rather flavorless but thick soup. One of the compassionate inmates of the cabane offered us some spaghetti. Norbert's eyes lit up until he heard Rony graciously decline the kind offer. It was getting late, and cooking the spaghetti would have meant another hour before we got to bed. We all went to sleep with visions of spaghetti dancing in our heads. Life's simplest pleasures are vastly magnified in the mountains!

Breakfast at three consisted of more tea without sugar, more stale bread, the remains of the dried meat, and a tasty but undersized wedge of Brie cheese. This meant each of us had one pear and two thirds of a bar of chocolate left to nourish us during the climb.

We left the hut at four thirty, the night cloudy, but moonlit. We climbed back up the rocky spine above the hut, thankful for the moon, which spared us using our lanterns and left both hands free for the climbing. Soon we were above the rocks and, strapping on our crampons, we climbed the ice ridge, which was far easier in ascent than it had been in descent. On we marched, trudging over névés and scrambling over easy rocks. Crampons were required once again as Rony chopped steps across an ice slope, giving all due respect to a tremendous cornice overhanging on our right. After an hour or two of mixed climbing, we came to the base of the *grand gendarme,* an imposing obstacle to be encountered at over four thousand meters!

The serious climbing began. We were in great form and were blessed with absolutely dry rock. Rony's judgment of the mountain's condition had been unerring. There followed two hours of beautiful rock climbing, nowhere difficult but always requiring careful attention. We were on belay almost continuously throughout this section, basically climbing slabs on the west face, just left of the actual ridge. From time to time we traversed gendarmes on the actual crest. It took little mental effort to imagine how difficult these rocks could be when iced.

To our left, the west face fell away steeply to the Manzettes Glacier and the chalets of Bricolla far, far below. Across from us, forming the other boundary of

Norbert Kaltenkirchen on the south ridge of the Dent Blanche

the west face, the Ferpècle ridge sprung up in soaring steps. The weather, which had been threatening below, now gave every indication that it would hold. We continued our upward course. Gendarme followed gendarme, and the climbing itself was so interesting that we were in no hurry to finish up. All too soon the serious climbing was over.

The top of the south ridge was anticlimactic, since for the last half hour we could almost walk with our hands in our pockets. By nine thirty we were "over" our peak. There were two other parties on top, while three others were threading their way toward the summit cross.

The first object to catch our eyes was the fearsome Viereselsgrat—the "Four Donkeys" ridge. It has an evil reputation for its double cornices,* and looking down on it from the summit, we certainly felt its reputation well earned. The Zmutt and Italian ridges on the Matterhorn were seen to particular advantage nearby, as were the sharp east ridge and imposing north face of the Dent d'Hérens. Far below us was the Col de Zinal and the Pointe de Zinal. Behind rose the Obergabelhorn, the Zinal Rothorn, and the ever-impressive Weisshorn. Indeed, all of the peaks of the Valais were visible, as well as Mont Blanc and other more distant peaks.

By unanimous vote, we decided to eat our chocolate on the summit and save our fruit and most of the tea for the recrossing of the glacier. Our "meal" concluded, we then set out for the Schönbühl, our prompt start encouraged by some ominous clouds hovering around the Dent d'Hérens.

Norbert led down, with Rony protecting us from behind as is customary for a guide. Norbert climbed beautifully, and, thanks to his surefooted lead, the difficult rock section was descended without incident. The weather turned fine once again, and we were able to appreciate fully the spectacular and savage beauty around us. There were many halts—to remove crampons, to change clothes, to take pictures, to drink a little tea, to point out a past climb or a future attempt. It was a rare time for all of us. We were perfectly happy—with our environment, with one another, with ourselves. Even the miseries of the Wandfluh were unable to alter our mood. We happily hurled yodels against the enclosing rock walls and looked back at our peak. By three thirty we were drinking hot tea and then beer at the Schönbühl. On empty stomachs, our spirits soared even higher as we consumed the beer.

---

* An overhanging mass of snow or ice above a steep slope or at the side of a ridge.

Back in Zermatt, Rony returned to his wife and newborn daughter; Norbert and I made plans for a celebration dinner. All of us hated to see this perfect day end. My own happiness would have been greatly diminished if I had known at the time that bad weather was to make all climbing impossible for the next two weeks. Never question a guide's judgment about the weather. Rony had picked the last day of the season on which it was possible to climb the Dent Blanche!

Unpleasant as my experience with Herr Doktor had been, the climb with Norbert more than made up for it. I had found a new friend. We had dinner together every night until we left Zermatt. His English was as bad as my German, but somehow we had no communication problems. In later years, we rendezvoused in Zermatt, hiking, climbing, eating, and drinking together. Today, Norbert is one of my best friends on or off a rope.

Chapter 8

Climbs at Home

While the Alps captured my dreams and a few weeks of my time each summer, most of my hours in the mountains were spent in New York, Vermont, and New Hampshire.

In 1964 I joined the Appalachian Mountain Club's New York chapter. Every weekend during the spring and fall I went on hikes either Saturday or Sunday, sometimes both. There were a variety of hikes offered, ranging from easy six- to seven-mile rambles to twenty-five-mile struggles through hilly if not truly mountainous terrain. One of the latter—a complete traverse of the Suffern–Bear Mountain Trail—particularly sticks in my mind.

The trip was led by Dave Ingalls, a well-known Eastern rock-climber and mountaineer. A party of six, including Dave, showed up for this twenty-five-mile toughie. Dave tore up the first hill, leading us all a rapid pace. One woman dropped out immediately. For seventeen miles, the rest of us crossed minor peaklets and rises in the plateau. Our pace was slightly faster than comfortable without being truly tiring. Since we were in the woods most of the time, I didn't regret the lack of opportunity to admire the view. At lunchtime—the seventeen-mile mark was by a highway—another of our group dropped out. You could hardly call her "soft" after seventeen miles, but I began to feel the hike was turning into a survival-of-the-fittest laboratory!

Four of us finished the hike, arriving at the Bear Mountain Inn well after dark despite our seven A.M. start and lack of rest stops. There is a special reward in pushing oneself like this, but I prefer to limit these tests to once or twice a year, as reassurance that legs and lungs still function properly.

I met a number of interesting people on the AMC hikes and to this day remain grateful to the club for broadening my new horizons. Before long, I was asked to lead hikes and was happy to do so. Leaders had different criteria for a successful hike. There was, for example, the "more the merrier" group leader, who led relatively easy walks advertising ease of access by public transportation, delightful bars at trail's end, special treats to be provided by the leader, and so forth. I still remember a hike on Schunemunk Mountain in which sixty-three mountain walkers participated. It seemed that the front of the caravan was halfway home before the rear of the column even started. These were the walks I soon learned to avoid.

As a leader, I always chose more strenuous trips, always inaccessible by public transportation. This way, people had to call for driving instructions or to ask for a ride, and I could control the size of the group and determine the ability of the applicants. There is nothing worse than leading a group of people whose ideas of a "good pace" are miles apart. The fast ones complain of being constantly held back, while the slower ones gasp their dissatisfaction with the unreasonable pace. When there is a gap, you must always favor the slower ones.

Over the years, I have also sponsored a number of applicants for the Appalachian Mountain Club. Within the club, they can receive instruction and participate in backpacking, rock-climbing, skiing (both downhill and cross-country), white-water canoeing. The AMC has chapters from Maine to Georgia. In most other parts of our country there are similar organizations that make it possible to learn about the mountains from those who already know and love them. A few of these groups are listed at the end of the book.

Through my business, I made the acquaintance of Al Zesiger. Al had lived in San Francisco for a number of years and was a member of the Sierra Club. He was a strong skier, enjoyed hiking, and had also done some climbing in Zermatt. We became immediate friends and for the last seven years have been on countless mountain trips together.

First there were trips up to Vermont, to revisit Mount Mansfield. One day stands out. It was a clear, cool October morning. Down in the Stowe Valley, the trees wore their brightest autumnal colors. We left our lodge at seven o'clock, had a quick breakfast, and headed out to the mountain. Around us was the rich profusion of blazing reds, oranges, and yellows. Above, the mountain was coated with white—the result of a heavy frost. We decided on the Bear Pond Trail, which climbs steeply up from Smuggler's Notch. At first, it winds in and out of steep cliffs, then runs through a beautiful pine forest. Here the deep green was highlighted by the diamond brilliance of the frost covering the tops of every tree. The sky was cloudless—a deep azure—and a light breeze enabled us to mount swiftly without so much as a drop of perspiration. On the summit, even the scrub brush and the lichen-covered rocks were coated with white. We were alone on the trail and felt in perfect harmony with our surroundings.

There were trips to the Camel's Hump, the only

four-thousand-foot peak in Vermont to escape the scourge
of the ski area developer. The trail we followed rose
gently through the woods before passing two beaver
ponds. Gray stumps, rising from the water, perforated
the otherwise unspoiled reflection of the summit pyramid
that towered several thousand feet above, two miles
away. Immediately above the lakes, cliffs soared several
hundred feet into the sky. The trail led steeply around
and up the cliffs and followed along a rocky ridge covered with blueberries. The berries slowed us down considerably. Then we entered the woods again, finally
reemerging at the base of the summit cone, rising above
us in the mist like the prow of a battleship. As is so
often the case in the mountains, the pitch proved less
formidable than it looked. On top there was no view, so
we descended quickly with an added incentive to return.

A new world awaited me in New Hampshire. Long
before I knew how to ski, I had gone with a group of
friends to Tuckerman's Ravine on Mount Washington.
One look at the famous Headwall convinced me that I
would devote myself to hiking that weekend. Later, I
made a winter ascent with two equipment fiends, who
raced up in little more than two hours. There were a few
anxious moments as we hurried under the *séracs* (ice
pinnacles) of the Right Gully before emerging on the
summit snowfields. Being somewhat less of an equipment
bug, I found my feet and legs thoroughly soaked when
we stopped on the summit. One of my companions insisted that we wait while he changed into his fishnet
socks and ate some dehydrated enzymes. Having neither
extra socks nor spare enzymes, I nearly froze!
Some years later I returned with Charlie Walker
and John McCabe, two friends from New York. All of us
had skied a great deal that winter, but now it was May,

The Camel's Hump

and all of us were out of shape. To ski the Headwall, you must first hike in 2.4 miles to the base of Tucker-man's Ravine, which is a vertical rise of two thou-sand feet—equal to the vertical drop of such well-known areas as Stowe and Mad River. From there the steep climbing begins—first to the "Lunch Rocks," about half-way up, and then up the Headwall itself. By the time we reached the "Lunch Rocks," John declared himself *hors de combat.* Charlie and I, after appropriate jibes at John about the importance of conditioning, continued about halfway up the Headwall. We strapped on our skies on an uncomfortably narrow ledge on the forty-five-degree slope, then pointed them downward. Or, rather, sideward. We traversed to the right for hundreds of feet, trying to build up courage for our first turns. Our stiff lower legs betrayed our fear. A few awkward lunges passed for turns. We didn't fall despite our tech-nical collapse. Before we could rave to John about what he had missed, he informed us that he had observed the entire fiasco, which bore little resemblance to skiing!

Our spirits revived with a long luncheon in the sun, continuous dosages of Rhine wines, and quick suppres-sion of our lack of accomplishments. That night, back at Whitney's Lodge in Jackson, we decided to forget our skis on Sunday and simply hike up the mountain. We planned to follow Boott Spur, the long rocky ridge that rises to the left of the Headwall. You then cross the top of the ravine and follow gentle slopes to the summit. John had done some hiking, and all of us ran laps around Central Park to keep in shape. We expected no problems.

The only problem was that we didn't make it! We marched without difficulty through the wooded slopes above Pinkham Notch. Once we rose above the treeline, however, the conditions changed radically. A tremendous wind smote us. Our parkas flapped and rattled like machine guns. For those who are not acquainted with Mount Washington, I should mention that it is the recipient of some of the world's worst weather. Winds in excess of two hundred miles per hour have been recorded on its summit. Snowstorms can develop in a matter of minutes, even in the middle of the summer. Although it is only slightly more than six thousand feet, people have died of exposure on its slopes with alarming regularity. Signs are liberally planted all over the mountain, warning the hiker to turn back at the slightest indication of bad weather. We got to the junction with the Boott Spur link and decided to go down to Hermit Lake at the foot of the ravine.

We congratulated each other on our prudence, but were somewhat disconcerted by a solitary hiker in shorts and T-shirt who walked on, unmindful of the fierce gale. Our chagrin was intensified at the Hermit Lake shelter, where a forest ranger was telling two twelve-year-olds that it would be all right to go on to the summit! Clearly, the weekend had not been one of extraordinary accomplishment. But, as is so often the case in the mountains, the effort is its own reward. Charlie, John, and I became close friends, shared two beautiful days, and immediately started to plan future White Mountain rambles.

Gradually, a group of mountain lovers was forming. Al Zesiger, investment adviser, was a constant companion. Charlie Walker, New York attorney, showed great interest in hiking and skiing trips to New Hampshire. John and Mary-Ann McCabe (he an attorney, she an anthropologist) hiked and skied as well as climbed in Zermatt. Dave Robison, globe-trotting free-lance writer and photographer, came whenever his work permitted. Surrounded by urban blight, smog, crime in the streets and other unhealthy distractions, we nevertheless used New York as our planning center for trips to the mountains. As often as not, two or more of us managed to be together on weekends, enjoying the varied charms of the New England mountains.

As Al and I got to know each other better, and as our mutual trust grew, big plans developed. One of our friends—John Valenstein—had crossed the Alps on skis in 1968. As we listened to tales of John's adventures and watched his films, Al and I decided we could do no less. The Haute Route became our big project in 1969!

Chapter 9

Saas Fee to Chamonix—
A New Dimension
in Skiing

In 1966, Al had first taken me down the expert slopes at Mad River Glen—his skis comfortably parallel, mine in a wobbly snow plow! I had survived this survival-of-the-fittest struggle, which actually marked the beginning of our friendship. Three years later, my snow plow had become a confident stem with occasional flashes of parallelism. When we'd first casually talked about the Haute Route, I'd thought my lack of technique would be a definite drawback. But the more people we questioned, the more apparent it became that strength and endurance counted far more than elegant style. Yes, a strong stem turn would carry me across the Alps!

One of the great delights of any adventure is the anticipation and planning. Al and I decided a year ahead of time that we would do the Haute Route with Rony. During the summer of 1968, I bought topographical maps and reviewed them with Rony, sketching out our proposed route in pencil. Rony had made the trip a number of times, and his vivid descriptions of the breathtaking scenery we would see made the maps come alive! Then, at home, Al and I reviewed the maps, talked to anyone we could find who had made the trip, and gradually started to assemble our equipment. Here, John Valenstein was invaluable. Not only was he a fine skier who had traversed the Haute Route, but he also had spent endless hours investigating the different types of equipment available. Al and I were only too happy to accept his advice as to type of skis (soft), bindings (adjustable cables), spare parts, clothing, and various other items.

We planned to ski as much as possible that winter of 1968-1969, conditioning our legs for the work ahead. In the early spring I was to start running every day, working my way up to five or six miles a day, in order to build up wind and stamina. My plans were abruptly curtailed, however, on January 14, when I fell in a dash for the subway, severely spraining my ankle. The mountain climber had come a cropper on the flat streets of New York!

For a week I lay in bed, the pain so excruciating that the doctor had to come twice to give me injections on top of the pills I was already taking. When I fell, my first thought was that I would be unable to ski the following weekend. During my stay in bed, the seriousness of the injury cast doubts on the entire winter—and the Haute Route! After that week, I was sent to Leon Root, a leading orthopedic surgeon in New York. Lee told me that a cast would immediately relieve the pain, but would involve a considerably longer rehabilitation period, since my muscles would atrophy in the plaster. I held my breath as I asked his professional opinion as to the possibility of leaving on May 3 for the Haute Route. While he could make no promises, he held out enough hope so that I immediately elected the pain and rejected the cast.

I was on crutches for another five weeks, several times fearing further injury as they slipped on the icy sidewalks of New York. But by the end of February I was walking on my own and exercising like a maniac. Four weeks later—the end of March—I was back at Stowe on skis!

The first weekend went well. I stuck to the intermediate trails, gradually regaining the feeling of the skis. I skied by myself the entire weekend, so that I would not be tempted by my friends to ski faster or take the steeper trails. The second weekend, Al accompanied me. We were both eager to take the tougher runs, feeling this would be good training for the Haute Route, despite the fact that we had been assured there were no tough spots. Charlie Lord, Hay Ride, Nose Dive, Lift Line, National—we worked our way up to the most difficult runs. And then we went behind the fence that blocks off the Starr, or International, one of the steepest runs to be found.

On my first turn I caught an edge. I sat gently back and into the hill. That was the right way to fall. The next thing I knew I was shooting down the thirty-five to forty-degree slope on my stomach, feet first. A flip and I was on my back, now sliding headfirst. I hit a few moguls and bounced, spun, and somersaulted through the air. In dread, I waited for the inevitable crack which would accompany my hitting a tree! Suddenly I had stopped. Later estimates on the length of my fall ranged from five to seven hundred feet. I lay there, afraid to move. Perhaps the shinbone was not connected to the anklebone, or the thigh bone to the hip bone! When I finally gathered the courage to move, everything seemed miraculously connected!

Plans were now firm. The orthopedist had wished me godspeed. Last-minute discussions with our friend John stretched out into hours. Missing equipment was purchased. We were off!

As the "little red train" brought Al and me closer to Zermatt, we were lost in our private thoughts. The high peaks—many of them old friends—gradually revealed themselves. First the mighty Mischabels, which split the valleys of Zermatt and Saas Fee, then the Weisshorn, magnificent in its isolation. Finally the Zermatt Breithorn burst into view and we knew we were home once more.

The Alps in the spring are quite different from the Alps of the "high" seasons, winter and summer. In those seasons, when the Alpine centers are choked with humanity, there is a hustle and bustle that almost belies the serenity of the surrounding peaks. As soon as we disembarked in Zermatt, we saw the difference. In summer, one is immediately greeted by "taxis"—horse and buggy—from dozens of Zermatt's hotels, as well as by a host of independent drivers. Now there were only three or four teams at the station. As is our custom, we declined assistance and walked up the narrow street as quickly as our bags, rucksacks, skis, ice axes, and extra boots would permit us. We settled ourselves in the ever-popular Walliserhof Hotel, where Herr Welschen has welcomed mountain lovers for more years than I can remember.

It was four o'clock and there was no time to lose. We hoped to start our trip on Monday, and we knew the stores would be closed on Sunday. We had two and a half hours to buy all the special items of equipment we hadn't brought over with us.

Our first stop was Rony's house. A few words of greeting and the three of us were off on a whirlwind tour of Zermatt's sporting goods shops. A new ice ax and crampons for Al, skins for our skis, spare pole baskets and cables for our bindings in case of emergency, lightweight flashlights, extra straps for our rucksacks, glacier goggles, gaiters, special sun cream for our lips. A couple of days in the mountains most likely would provide painful reminders of any items we had overlooked!

Sunday was rainy, but it didn't really matter. It was our "rest day," set aside to synchronize our bodies with European time. A short walk up to Zmutt was our only acclimatization, but it provided Al with a good laugh when I confessed to three blisters from my soft boots bought specially for the Haute Route—good work for two hours!

Monday was an exact repetition of Sunday—heavy rain and low-lying clouds. A brief council of war was held. We had intended to start in Argentière, France, and take the northern route back to Zermatt and Saas Fee. This route, traveled less frequently, involves more real mountaineering than the classical east-to-west traverse—the southern route—which starts in Saas Fee and finishes by crossing Mont Blanc from Courmayeur in Italy to Chamonix. In any event, no party had made the Haute Route in either direction by the time we arrived, due to exceptionally bad weather during the last two weeks of April. Because of the unusually heavy snowfall and subsequent avalanche danger on the northern route, Rony advised that we abandon our original plans and head for Saas Fee.

With the weather showing little cause for hope, we nevertheless took the eleven o'clock train to Stalden, where we had time for a hurried lunch before boarding the "post autobus" up to Saas Fee.

Saas Fee! How many happy climbing holidays had included a visit to this village, surrounded by an awe-inspiring glacial cirque.* We had always been blessed by sun before, but on May 5 it was raining heavily in the village and huge banks of clouds hung low over the valley,

---

* A natural amphitheater in the mountains.

concealing the steep rock walls we knew towered above. There was little cause for hope, but having ridden the train and the bus, we couldn't commit ourselves to the return journey without giving it a good try. Besides, thanks to a brand-new cable car, the Britannia Hut was now merely an hour's walk from the lift terminus.

The scene that greeted us when we stepped out of the upper station was unforgettable. A blizzard was howling, with winds of fifty to sixty miles per hour and the visibility little more than a ski length. On the optimist's theory that the weather must get better, we triumphed over reason and set out for the hut.

An ordinarily short and pleasant stroll became an intense struggle. The hours seemed like half a day. Our

The Haute Route—Italian Alps seen from near Valpelline

The Haute Route—descending from the Col de Fenêtre to the
snowline above Vaud

goggles were almost immediately frozen over, and the
wind and snow had covered all traces of earlier tracks.
When we finally reached the hut, the gale was so intense
that we literally had to crawl up the steps leading to salvation inside. We saw a couple of friendly faces—Alphonse
Franzen and Ricky Andenmatten—Zermatt guides who
had arrived with clients a day earlier and were determined
to sit out the storm. In fact, the Britannia Hut was packed
with about fifty eager skiers, all hoping that the weather
would permit them to cross the Adler pass the next day.
As we prepared for bed after an ample meal, the intensity
of the wind increased. Determined to visit the WC—about
a hundred feet away—before retiring, we were stopped

somewhat short of our mark by the elements. Later discussion convinced us that we weren't the only ones not up to this treacherous traverse!

Tuesday was almost an exact repetition of Monday; there was less wind, but the snow was falling even more heavily. There was no question of continuing; our suggestion to perhaps wait another day or two was countered with the tale of two Swiss, who had recently been rescued from the Hollandia Hut, where they had been snowed in for eight days.

Our caravan was something to behold. Fifty skiers—laden with crampons, ice axes, and ropes, as well as the usual rucksacks and ski gear—were strung out in one long column as we passed anxiously under some avalanche-prone gullies. We pointed our skis downward in the direction of Saas. For one used to the "packed powder" (ice) of Vermont, the knee-deep heavy powder was a delightful reminder of human frailty. "Parallel" lost its meaning as I struggled down the relatively gentle slopes. As we got lower, the snow got heavier and heavier . . . and heavier! To ensure our humility, rocks started cropping up with increasing frequency! Finally we were picking our way through the forest—rocks, tree stumps, branches, and snow the consistency of household cement.

All this time, the snow was coming down in large wet flakes. Steaming from my exertions in the heavy stuff, I took off my down parka and actually enjoyed a natural shower! When we finally reached the Walliserhof Hotel in Saas Fee, we were a sorry lot—all of us drenched to the skin. The rest rooms were soon converted into locker rooms, and everyone tried changing into the driest clothes he or she could find.

Our spirits, however, weren't dampened at all. We were aware that we had lived an unforgettable twenty-four hours, even if our efforts weren't crowned with success. And double orders of "grog" around the table turned dinner into a half-dressed revel.

When Wednesday, in Zermatt, showed no signs of improving weather, Al and I held another council of war. We had firm commitments to be in Milan a week from that day, and time was running out. After a long and careful consideration of the alternatives (elapsed time—about seventeen seconds!) we canceled our plans, wrote the affected parties, and dug in, determined to triumph over the weather with a virtuoso display of patience.

Wednesday and Thursday were stormy, although I managed to get an extreme sunburn while skiing on Wednesday at the Furgsattel a mile above Zermatt. I have since learned never to ski unprotected, even when there seems to be little or no sun. Finally, the weather report on Friday was for clearing and better weather. To look up from Zermatt was to disbelieve the forecast. Saas Fee was out of the question in such marginal conditions, but we might set out directly from Zermatt. With some misgiving, we took the nine thirty cable car to Schwarzsee at the foot of the Matterhorn. Dense clouds, snow, almost no visibility. Anyone who has climbed in high mountains knows the agonies of decision-making when the atmospheric conditions are uncertain.

"Nothing ventured, nothing gained"—we were off, poling our way in the direction of Maria zum Schnee, the little chapel at the edge of the lake. Then down over breakable crust toward Stafelalp. With the mists swirling around us and the Matterhorn's bulk lurking somewhere in the clouds above, we were in another world just ten minutes from the cable-car terminus. As we picked our way gingerly through the treacherous snow, we saw several chamois in profile on the ridge above us. Soon we were at the bottom, our skins on our skis.

The walk up the Zmutt Valley to the Schönbühl Hut

The south face of the Obergabelhorn

is a gentle one. We kept to the left, close under the Matterhorn's mighty north face. After about an hour and a half
the sun came out—a spontaneous signal to do business
with Kodak. Cameras clicked madly and movie cameras
whirred. It was our first opportunity to capture some of
the marvelous mountain scenery. The Matterhorn's Zmutt
Ridge loomed over our heads, and the Dent d'Hérens, with
its mighty ice battlements, looked like a misplaced Himalayan giant.

Fifteen minutes later, the mists closed in. In fact, the
whereabouts of the Schönbühl Hut were somewhat in
question. We knew we had to cross the moraine at some
point, but just where to do so was the problem. Compasses
were brought into play, and Rony took a letter-perfect

reading. Little things like this distinguish the professional from the amateur!

A very steep traverse above the Schönbühl Glacier brought us to the hut, about three hours from Stafelalp. We were the sole occupants of the hut along with Ricky Andenmatten and two clients. The first order of business was to build a fire and to start melting snow for our cooking. In no particular order, tea, beer, cheese, dried fruit, dry meat, soup, sausage, and chocolate were consumed. Somehow we had forgotten to eat lunch, and we knew we would need all our strength for the next day's crossing to Arolla. Unfortunately, alternate chills and fever—the first result of my sunburn—deprived me of my normally robust appetite.

When dinner was over, the rituals of barometer tapping (the usual "do not tap" was, of course, ignored) and sky gazing were performed. Our cheeriest estimate for the morrow was "fifty-fifty." We consoled ourselves by assuring one another how much better it was to be up here in the mountains than down in the village. Everyone agreed so vehemently that I was relieved to sense that others shared my doubts.

We planned to leave at five o'clock on Saturday morning, but when we awoke at four it was snowing heavily. A lovely spring! The next time we turned over it was six o'clock and—wonder of wonders—it was clearing. Making haste slowly, we left the hut at seven thirty. We were to pay dearly for our late start.

Having skied down to the Tiefmatten Glacier, we secured our animal skins to our skis and started the climb around the Stockje and up toward the Col de Valpelline. Before long, we started to ascend an extremely steep snow wall. The snow was rotten, and, as each of the six of us passed, the track became more crumbly. The exposure, while not extreme in a mountaineering sense, was nevertheless more than we would have ordered with our skis. At one critical point near the top of the wall, Ricky and one of his clients engaged in a terse but desperate dialogue:

"Ricky!"

"Yah, Andy."

"Ricky, I'm having trouble!"

"Yah, Andy."

"Ricky, my downhill ski keeps slipping. I don't think I'm going to make it!"

"Yah, Andy. Just do the best what you can make."

"But, Ricky . . ."

"Yah, Andy."

Guides are not often well versed in the ways of mere mortals. However, the wall was surmounted and a rest was very much in order. After ten minutes we set out again for the col. It was mercilessly hot and we all performed a high-altitude striptease. I was so warm that I removed my gloves for about three hours. The blisters on my hands three days later were ample evidence of the sun's intensity.

Our immediate problem was the gluey condition of the snow. The guides changed the lead every fifty to a hundred steps, since breaking track was exhausting even for these mountain men. Meanwhile the leaden snow had managed to ball up between our skis and the skins. Our efforts were like those of a man walking uphill with his feet encased in blocks of cement. By the time we reached the Col de Valpelline it was twelve forty-five, and we still had a long way to go. Skins off. The snow on the Tsa de Tsan Glacier was abominable. Turns were a constant reminder of one's inadequacy. A short schuss and back on with the skins for the climb to the Col du Mont Brûlé. We passed a long line of ski tourers who had evidently been snowbound at the Vignettes Hut for several days.

As we climbed toward the col, the weather again took

a turn for the worse. In fact, when we reached our pass, visibility was less than two feet! The wind was roaring, whipping the snow in our faces. The mists boiled up from below, like a scene from Dante's Inferno. In retrospect, I'm glad the fog prevented us from seeing where we were going, the descent being as steep as from one of the gullies at Tuckerman's Ravine. We never varied our procedure: a carefully controlled side-slipping traverse and then a kick turn. At one point, the slope actually seemed like sixty-five to seventy degrees (I'm sure it wasn't) and I dangled by one rucksack strap held securely in Ricky's iron hand as I struggled to right myself after an improperly executed kick turn. This steep passage was soon over, and we descended gradually over the Upper Arolla Glacier. The clouds made it difficult to spot familiar landmarks, such as the Évêque and the Bouquetins, and the compass was reactivated.

The Lower Arolla Glacier held a spectacular surprise. The ordinary descent route had been totally obliterated by a massive avalanche from the north face of Mont Collon. (We learned later that the fall had occurred the day before our arrival.) Accordingly, we kept to the rocks high up on the right and then picked our way down onto the bottom of the glacier. Thanks to the unusual quantity of snow, we were able to ski to within a half mile of the village by five o'clock, in time for a well-earned if somewhat belated lunch.

After our little snack at trail's end, we trudged along the path to the tiny village of Arolla, which lies at the head of the right-hand branch of the Val d'Hérens above Sion in the Rhône Valley. It was still rainy and damp as we walked up to the Mont Collon Hotel. A famed hangout for mountain climbers in the summer, it was, unfortunately, shut at this season. A little farther up the hill—with skis cutting into tired shoulders—we learned that the other large hotel was filled to accommodate a local wedding. Finally, just as we were losing hope, the Hotel de la Poste welcomed us.

Here it was my turn to have a little laugh on Al. He had distinguished himself during the day, never once complaining while the rest of us suffered from sunstroke (myself), blistered feet (one of Ricky's clients), altitude (Ricky's other client) and excess weight (all of us except Al). However, our "good scout" had revealed his human shortcomings by expressing his longing for a hot bath while we were still high up on the Arolla Glacier. Several beers after our arrival at the hotel, Al instructed me to exercise my French in order to secure us a room with private bath.

"*Nous n'en avons pas, monsieur.*"

"Sorry, Al. No privates."

"Well, how about a semiprivate?"

"*Madame, avez-vous un semi-privé?*"

"*Non, monsieur.*"

"No go, Al."

"Well, find out where the bath on our floor is located. I'm ready."

"*Madame, où se trouve le bain à notre étage?*"

"*Je le regrette, monsieur, mais il n'y a pas de bains à l'hôtel.*"

"Al, would you believe no bath tonight?"

I hope the proprietress didn't understand Al's rich vocabulary. Supper was uninspired, but we needed little inspiration after almost eleven hours of hard work. Several bottles of wine later, we wandered off to sleep.

Sunday morning was a miracle. As we looked out the window, we could see the Pigne d'Arolla glittering in the sun. The Mont Collon, its precipitous north face staring right at us, pierced the blue sky. After the gloomy weather of the past week, the exquisite beauty of a perfect spring day in a remote valley of the high Alps was unbelievably refreshing. Before we were even dressed, our cameras were working overtime. In case there had been any doubt, it was great to be alive!

Breakfast was a leisurely affair. Our bill settled, we went out on the patio to rearrange our equipment. Again, we had to stop to admire the view. Unlike so many famous mountain resorts, which, in fact, lie at the foot of the mountains, Arolla seems to be in the very heart of the Alpine world. The Dents de Perroc, Aiguille de la Tsa, the Bouquetins, Mont Collon, the Pigne, the Aiguilles Rouges d'Arolla—all are visible from the village. While there are a number of high huts, including the Bertol and the Vignettes, most of Arolla's peaks may be climbed in a single day directly from the village.

Inertia was at an all-time high when at nine thirty the guides finally convinced us that it really was a long way to the Vignettes Hut—some four thousand vertical feet. In fact, when they pointed in the direction of our destination, it seemed a crime to take such a rare spring day and spoil it with so much hard work. We went all the same.

We had carried our skis for little more than a couple of hundred yards when we were able to strap them on and climb up little tongues of snow that came down to the very edge of the village. After emerging from the forest, we had to remove our skis again to cross a stream. Then we began the steep climb up to the Glacier de Pièce, which in turn leads gently to the Col des Vignettes and our destination, the Vignettes Hut. Our pace was unhurried. There were plenty of stops for picture-taking, and a much longer halt for lunch. At this point, we were rounding into shape and were able to enjoy fully our beautiful surroundings. A special appreciation of scenery follows hard work to an extent that can never be experienced from a train or cable car. We felt ourselves a part of the landscape, rather than merely observers. As we nibbled on chocolate and dried fruit and sipped our tea, a large group of skiers descended and shouted hearty greetings as they passed.

We arrived at the hut a little before three o'clock. We had broken no records in our leisurely ascent, but there was no need for hurrying on such a day. Situated at over ten thousand feet, the Vignettes Hut is perched on top of a spectacular precipice. Rather than having a door straight into the interior, there is a protective stone wall that prevents fatalities on the very threshold. The promenade to the WC is roped in for the same reason.

It had been a memorable day. In the midst of our jubilation, Ricky announced that he was performing major surgery: his client's heel blister had now spread to the circumference of a baseball and it was time to do something about it. After the snipping, each bronzed member of the hearty band proffered his own "foolproof" blister powder. Etiquette forbade turning down any of the kind offers, and the poor victim was almost obscured by the powder clouds.

The next morning, Monday, May 12, I became the victim, severe water blisters covering the better part of what had been my face. The fever and chills had abated at last, but I still wasn't finished with the hideous sunburn.

At six A.M. we were under way toward Italy, heading down the gentle Otemma Glacier. Forty-five minutes and six miles later we were negotiating the *schlucht*, the ice fall at the bottom of the glacier. Looking back toward the hut, we could see the sun now hitting the high peaks. Another perfect day!

As we strapped our skins onto our skis for the last time, Rony dropped a bombshell.

"Where are your passports?"

"You didn't tell us to bring them, Rony. We don't have them."

"How do you expect to cross three frontiers without them?"

"Well, certainly no one would suspect a bunch of skiers."

"Shall we go back the way we came—to avoid trouble?"

"What do you think?"

"You should have brought your passports."

"I have my Swiss Alpine Club card. Maybe that will help."

"What about you, Al?"

"I'd hate to spend the rest of my days held in detention by a French or Italian customs officer!"

"What shall we do? I have my passport."

"Let's chance it, Rony!"

Therefore, alone in the middle of a vast plateau, we stealthily crept up toward the Col de Fenêtre and Italy. The scenery soon made us forget our fears of an international incident. Behind us, the peaks of Arolla stood out, majestically, and in the far distance, the mighty pyramid of the Weisshorn pierced the sky. The Ruinette was directly behind us, and as we climbed up we could look back on the Otemma Glacier, which we had descended in its entirety before our normal breakfast hour at home.

The Col de Fenêtre is well named. It is truly a window between Switzerland and Italy, a narrow gap in the mountain chain. As we approached, the rugged cliffs of the Mont Gelé dominated the scene. Slowly but surely, as if drawn by a magnet, we approached the pass. It was hard to realize that we had been marching three hours without a halt when we finally reached our objective. No customs officers here!

Al and I agreed that the topping of this pass was

the highlight of the trip. Behind us stretched the Valais, miles and miles of ice, rock, and snow—the most impressive upthrust of the Swiss Alps. And before us another world, the world of the southern slope. Yes, Italy was bursting with green. Spring was no longer a promise in the air. It had been realized in grass and trees, in branch and flower and leaf. And beyond, snow again—the Graian Alps of Italy—the Grivola, the Gran Paradiso, the mountains of Cogne. We would have liked to have spent the entire day on this very spot, reliving the adventures of the past days. But after an hour's halt, Rony reminded us of the remoteness of our destination for the day—Courmayeur, nestled at the foot of Mont Blanc's awesome southern precipice. We pointed our skis downhill and were introduced to "spring snow," an inch or two of light, corn snow on top of a solid crust. Our yodels broke the stillness. This was truly the "freedom of the hills!" Each of us cut his own tracks, stopping often to look back and admire the patterns. However, this delight soon gave way to an almost flat stretch where the sun oppressed us mightily as we poled along, trying unsuccessfully to avoid breaking through. Here and there, roofs of shepherds' huts—occupied only in the summer—peeked through the snow. In just twenty minutes, the three of us were almost completely sapped. It must have been a hundred degrees, and the glare off the snow was terrific.

All at once, we were in the middle of a field, with no snow in sight. The problem was that we were still several thousand feet above the hamlet of Vaud. For a while it looked as though we were on the wrong side of an enormous ravine. There was snow on the other side, but no way of getting there. The thought of climbing up again was horrendous. Ever resourceful, Rony found a nearly vertical (or so it seemed) snow gully that hooked up with further ribbons of snow leading down to Vaud. Indulging his sadistic side, Al took lengthy footage of me as I gingerly sideslipped the difficult bit.

Finally we were skiing (or, to be accurate, sideslipping) down a gorge. It was still choked with snow and provided a direct, if somewhat steep approach to our objective. At last the snow turned to water, and we removed our skis to descend the path that ran alongside the waterfall. Beautiful fir trees and the open fields carpeted with spring flowers—crocuses, soldanella, dandelions—stretched ahead of us. It was hard to believe that six hours earlier we had set out from the Vignettes Hut into a world of ice and snow.

Al and I realized just how tired we both were when

The Trifthorn, Zinal Rothorn, and Weisshorn peaks seen from the summit of the Wellenkuppe

we both saw the same mirage. There it was, just ahead, a pure, sparkling mountain brook with a little inn beckoning just across the stream. We were dumbfounded when the mirage materialized as the "Cantina Glassier." During the following fifteen minutes this inn was the center of frenzied action. Beer, *coca*, and everything else liquid was poured down as though we had just crossed the Sahara. I then used my best Italian to negotiate for a taxi. Ten minutes—and four rounds of drinks—later, our man was there, smiling cheerfully, ready to take us through Ollomont and Valpelline to Aosta.

The countryside was breathtaking. Our road started deep in a narrow valley, but gradually the panorama widened, until finally the Italian Alps burst upon us. Contrasted against the lush forests, the flower-carpeted fields, and the orange-tiled roofs so typical of the Alpine countries, the mountains seemed unreal. Around each bend in the road a new and even more spectacular vista opened. Our driver—a true patriot—was pleased by our obvious enthusiasm and stopped often to permit more picture-taking.

Aosta was steaming, no buses were running to Courmayeur that day: it was a holiday. But taxis are unbelievably cheap by American standards, and we had soon hired one to take us to Courmayeur, or, to be precise, to the little village of Entrèves nestled above Courmayeur under the shadow of the Monarch of the Alps, "Monte Bianco."

Rony, who seems to know all the right places, directed us to the Albergo delle Funivie, just across the cobblestone street from the cable car that would take us the following morning high up on Mont Blanc to Pointe Hellbrunner, from where we would start our descent to Chamonix. It was now two thirty and time for a real meal.

Our hostess overwhelmed us with loaves of bread,

an enormous platter of cold cuts, two trays of antipasto, cheese, heaping bowls full of spaghetti bolognese, two whole chickens served cold, a couple of bottles of excellent local wine, an immense bowl of salad, and a tureen of fresh fruit compote. Two and a half hours later we staggered from the table. We walked around the entire town (elapsed time—three minutes), bought a few postcards, put our rather gamey clothes out to air, and retired to sleep off our gargantuan repast. At seven, Al was still fast asleep, but Rony and I decided to go out for a beer.

We found a little café that offered a great variety of urban pleasures, including a pinball machine. I challenged Rony, who promptly outscored me by a considerable margin.

"That was lucky, Rony."

"Shall we try again, Fred?"

Eleven games—and eleven losses—later, I began to suspect that one of the many qualifications necessary for becoming a guide must be the ability to earn international master points on the pinball circuit. Games concluded, we ate continuously until bedtime soon after ten o'clock. The next day was the Vallée Blanche, the end of our trip!

Tuesday, May 13, dawned bright and clear. We hurried to take the first lift at eight o'clock. There were a large number of fellow skiers—a few more than the car would comfortably hold—but "operation sardine" was under way. And despite being cramped throughout the journey, we were still awed by the panorama that greeted us on our arrival. To the south, the craggy ranges of the Italian Alps pierced the sky. Totally surrounded by mountains, Courmayeur lay at our feet. To the west lay the summit of Mont Blanc and its supporting peaks. Across from us, the Dent du Géant . . . and in front of us reared the verticality of the Chamonix Aiguilles.

Whoosh! Swish! Spring snow on the famous Vallée

Rony Inderbinen negotiating a difficult ice pitch on the Dent d'Hérens

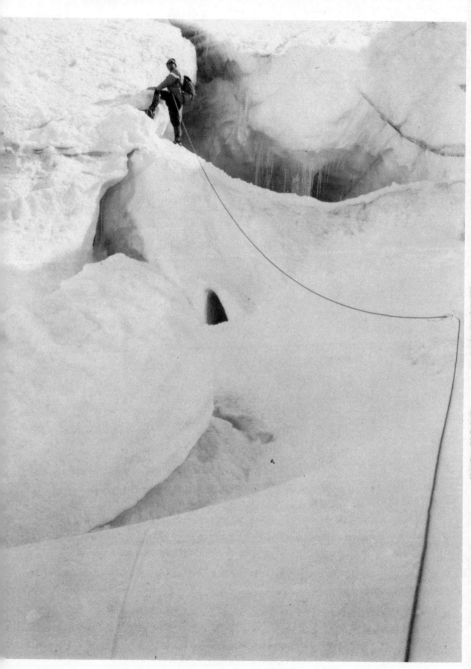

Séracs on the Mountet Glacier

The Haute Route—the final *séracs* on the Mer de Glace

Blanche. We resembled a band of skiing desperados. Al and I had masked our faces with our handkerchiefs to fight off the sun. Our dark glasses broke the monotony of the white handkerchiefs and our white sun hats. The sun had certainly gotten the best of us. Even Al ("I never get sunburned") resembled a charcoal fossil after five days of intense exposure.

Mont Maudit, Requin—the peaks whizzed by. And then we were in the ice fall. Snowplow, lunge, sideslip—the way was narrow and the crevasses, while narrow, were open and sobering to contemplate. And then we were past the *séracs*, ready to wax up for the final schuss of several miles across the Mer de Glace. Grépon, Grandes Jorasses, Dru . . . alternate bands of ice and slush required a survival technique, with no time for thoughts of elegant style.

Now we were at the foot of the Montenvers, regretfully removing our skis for the last time. The climb up to the train station was full of interest, steep, somewhat exposed and altogether difficult with our skis on our backs. At the station, we had time for three rounds of orange drinks before embarking for Chamonix. It was hard to believe our trip was over.

Not quite! Upon arrival in Chamonix, which was scorching hot, we learned that because of another holiday (this one French, not Italian), no buses were running to Martigny in Switzerland. The train schedule was such that we would be unable to reach Zermatt that night, even though it was now just a little after one o'clock! Once again, a taxi proved our salvation. We sailed through Argentière and over the frontier at Vallorcine. Our last exposure to the omnipresent customs men. I suppose we looked totally incapable of international intrigue, and the officer knew Rony from somewhere, so we made it to Switzerland. And, coming in, we went through the famous

Col de la Forclaz; although we'd heard a lot about the pass, we were totally unprepared for the view that greeted us as we topped it. At our feet lay Martigny and the Rhône Valley. To the right in the foreground was the Petit St. Bernard and farther back rose the peaks of the Simplon. North of the Rhône Valley, the continuous wall of the Oberland reared its snowy summits. It was a stunning, and fitting, climax to our circular journey.

Before the train left Martigny, we sat for a while on the patio outside the Buffet de la Gare. It was hard to place the previous five days in their proper perspective; only time would succeed in doing that. For Rony, it was an annual ritual—a renewing that has become part of his life cycle. For Al and me, it opened new horizons. We had combined our two great loves—climbing and skiing. For the three of us, we had all enjoyed the special friendship that mountain travel encourages.

After our crossing of the Alps, I came to have a deeper appreciation of the moral and philosophical excellence of the "bear who went over the mountain." May there always be another mountain!

Chapter 10

A Word About Conditioning

I am not a doctor. Nor am I a highly skilled athlete who has undergone the rigors of a carefully organized training table. Countless books and articles have been written about aerobics, calisthenics, diet, exercise, and training regimes. While I have nothing to add to this, I feel it might be helpful to share some of the observations I have made from firsthand experience.

It was painfully obvious to me way back in 1959 that physical fitness played an important role in climbing. Technique was essential, but was not enough in and by itself. In any sport, you must be in excellent shape to be at the top. But most sports, to be enjoyed on the recreational level, require relatively little training. I have found climbing an exception.

Let me use skiing—a sport I know well and love—as an example. To be sure, the first few days of a new season are tentative. I tend to ski easier trails, ski more slowly and for a shorter period of time than later in the season. Yet from the first day on I can enjoy myself. Most years, I have tried to do limbering-up exercises for six to eight weeks prior to skiing, but even this regime has often been sloppy.

However, skiing is not really tiring. Obviously, racers require tremendous stamina, and the recreational skier who wants to push himself will sleep well at night. But even without any waiting in line for a lift (a rare event), you will get a chance to rest as you ride up the lift. Climbing involves more continuous effort, a greater energy output, and it makes more severe demands on legs, lungs, and heart.

Enough of the problems! How should you prepare yourself for climbing? I have always felt natural exercise (enjoyed for itself rather than merely as preparation for something else) is the best answer. Obviously, hiking is an ideal preparation (from a conditioning, not a technical, point of view). Physiologically, it is particularly difficult for us to lift our bodies vertically, which is what we do when we walk up hills, whatever their steepness. And the best way to get ready for this type of exercise is to do it!

Most of my hiking is done around New York or in Vermont or New Hampshire. After the ski season, I usually start gradually, with hikes of six to eight miles. After a couple of these, I try somewhat longer trips, of ten to fourteen miles. Finally, I usually plan at least one "push" —anywhere from eighteen to twenty-five miles. All the while I seek out gradually steeper terrain and slowly but surely increase my walking pace. Temperature is a critical factor—the hotter it is, the more painful the training.

This kind of hiking is great, but has several limitations from my point of view. First of all, like most working people, I can only go on weekends, which means not often enough. And, having other obligations from time to time, I am lucky if I can hike every other weekend. Second, unless I really force the pace, I do not push my lungs enough to prepare them for the greater demands of high-altitude climbing. Few of my friends want to push, as there's little or no reason to do so unless you are preparing for bigger and better things. To go fifteen to twenty miles alone is, in my opinion, unduly risky. Even a veteran can turn an ankle, as I did in the streets of New York!

In any training program, I believe three ingredients are essential—regularity, a gradual build-up, and discipline. My answer has been running. I came upon it quite by accident. One spring, seven years ago, I was some ten pounds overweight as my summer vacation approached. I though I could "run it off." I live very close to Central Park, and I decided to go out after work and do a lap around the 1.58-mile track encircling the reservoir. At first I found it necessary to alternate jogging and walking; then I gradually increased the number of steps I ran before walking a hundred steps. By the end of the second week I was running two laps, nonstop. Although I lost no weight (other than climbing, I find the only way to lose weight is to cut down my food intake), I found myself in better shape by the time I arrived in Switzerland than in previous years. Now I start earlier and gradually build up to five to six miles per day. Usually I try to run eight to twelve miles at least once before leaving for my trips. I find this regime satisfies the requirements outlined above, and, furthermore, whereas at first it was merely a preparatory discipline, I now look forward to running. Besides building up legs and lungs, running has other benefits. It is a great way to work off the tensions of the workday. It takes a little longer than a couple of martinis, but seems eminently healthier. It is difficult to feel tense after running five miles. I start running in April and continue until I leave for the Alps in June. Three times a week is my target, in addition to whatever exercise I can get on weekends, such as hiking, swimming, or tennis. My friend Al likes running so much that he now runs the year round.

Sun protection on the Mer de Glace

There are many days when I don't feel like running, but I gain a certain strength from forcing myself. There is a thin line between self-discipline and compulsion. I *think* I'm on the right side of that line, and I *know* it helps me. There are times when I'm running when I feel like quitting, not so much from fatigue but from simple boredom. Going on despite this reinforces my self-image, builds my self-confidence. Very often, I have experienced similar "boredom fatigue" on prolonged glacier marches. Having built up a reservoir of "I can do it" feelings from running, I cash in a few points to overcome the problem.

Self-confidence is important in most big undertakings, and climbing is no exception. In climbing, you need to have confidence in your physical self, and running has done this for me. I am neither graceful nor exceptionally well coordinated. But by running—far rather than fast— I create an inner strength. To be sure, once a week, I do time myself. As with any repeated exercise, progress is almost inevitable. And with improving times for the various distances comes improving morale. In climbing, of course, feeling capable of doing the thing is all-important. Just as the mind needs to be active each day and seeks to accomplish, so, too, does the physical self need continuous proof of its vitality! In running as in climbing, you quickly learn your own limits. Expectations, while optimistic, become realistic. I have a feeling that long-distance swimming provides many of the same benefits as running, though, I must admit I'm partial to the latter. Whatever your choice, build yourself up—mentally and physically. And don't start too fast!

I also do some simple calisthenics that emphasize stretching and arm strength. Push-ups, overhand chins, twenty-five-pound weights for one-armed curls—these are the principal exercises for the arms. Simple yoga exercises generally suffice for producing adequate agility (again I am talking about nonacrobatic climbing!).

One rule I've found increasingly useful is to hit your peak three to four weeks ahead of your trip. The reason is simple. When your body is under peak physical pressure is when you are most likely to develop tangible protests—bursitis, tendonitis, shin splints, and so forth. Thanks to the expert ministrations of my sympathetic and highly skilled orthopedist, Barry Watson, none of these maladies has ever prevented me from climbing. Soaking in hot water, three days of rest, a week without physical exercise, a shot of cortisone—one or a combination of Dr. Watson's prescribed treatments has always put me back in shape before departure for the Alps. However, a relatively minor condition, aggravated a few days

before departure date, can absolutely ruin a climbing holiday.

So, train hard and hit your peak early! Finally, find
an orthopedist who understands and is sympathetic to the
compulsions of mountain madness!

Chapter 11

How I Didn't Climb the Weisshorn and Loved Every Minute of Not Doing It

"The Weisshorn isn't a mountain you just *do*. It has to be courted." So said Rony's wife, Stephanie, during the summer of 1970, one of many seasons in which we didn't do the Weisshorn.

Since 1959 I have missed only one season of climbing in and around Zermatt. Around 1966 I began to dream of someday doing all its thirty-seven "four-thousanders," that is, peaks of four thousand meters (13,123 feet). Since that time, the Weisshorn—perhaps the most beautiful peak in the Alps—had been a constant topic of conversation. We planned to climb it in 1968. The last week of August, we climbed the Trifthorn, the Pollux, and the Nordend on the Monte Rosa. September was "always the best weather," and with these three training climbs under my belt and two weeks of climbing ahead of me, the Weisshorn appeared to be in the bag—except that it rained and snowed twelve of the first fourteen days in September!

Since 1969 was devoted to the Haute Route, the Weisshorn had to wait until 1970. There was no question as to what our major target was this year. A few "warm-ups" and then . . .

August 15 was arrival date in Zermatt, and the following day Rony and I were already scrambling around the friendly crags of the Riffelhorn. We started up the Skyline Ridge. There is a short, steep wall with rather thin holds near the top where year after year I scuffle clumsily and finally retreat into an easier chimney to the left. This time I climbed the wall direct, in good form—an unbelievably small accomplishment, but, I thought, a highly favorable omen of things to come. We spent three hours on some of the well-known routes, and I took a series of photos as I followed Rony up the *Steil Eck*—the "Steep Edge." Finally, after a more difficult climb up the *Mittel Eck*, we headed down.

On August 18, at noon, we met at the railroad station —Rony, Herr Professor Wangerin, another client, and myself. We were going to try for the Dom, the highest mountain totally in Switzerland and the third highest in Europe. The Dom is not technically difficult, being a long snow hike, but that hike is *very* long! A half hour later the train deposited us in the heat of Randa, just a few miles from Zermatt.

Bad news! After two weeks of bad weather, it appeared that there was a waiting list at the Dom Hut. In fact, there were close to seventy climbers who would have to share sleeping accommodations for forty! The hut is a full five thousand feet above Randa. Even with the hundreds of feet of fixed cables and numerous pitons in place, the walk to the hut is surely one of the steepest and most tiring in all of Switzerland. What's more, the weather report was somewhat less than optimistic. The prospect of a hard walk, a night on the floor, and a less than fifty-

The Weisshorn seen from the summit of the Zinal Rothorn

The Weisshorn with the Täschalp Chapel in the foreground

fifty chance of making our climb combined to negate our plans. In an altogether atypical demonstration of Valaisian flexibility, Rony agreed that we should return to Zermatt. Upon arrival we sneaked up the back street to the Trockener Steg Bahn. Our new plan was to spend the night at the Theodul Hut and try for Castor—one of the Twins—on the following day. At least if the bad weather did materialize, we had only a short hour's walk up to the hut and down again.

Prominently displayed outside our room in the hut was the sign *Attenzione ai Mozzicone*. We thought this meant "Beware of Bedbugs" and had a rather troubled sleep (we later learned it meant "Beware of Cigarette Butts!"). In the end, however, we had a longer rest than anticipated, since when we first rose at four o'clock the weather was totally unsuitable for climbing. We returned to Zermatt.

Even in defeat, it had been a happy experience. Professor Wangerin a man of about sixty, was a delightful companion, and it was good to see that if one takes reasonable care of one's body and is given good health, one can climb even at that age.

Thursday, August 20, was another depressing day for climbers. Low-lying clouds precluded thoughts of high climbs, but Rony and I decided to get up early on Friday, take the lifts up to Blauherd, walk to Fluhalp, and from there have a go at the Schwarz Grat. The ridge is low, nowhere exceeding eleven thousand feet, and is all rock, as its name implies. It runs essentially east to west, connecting the Pfulwe of the Rimpfischhorn with the Ober Rothorn.

Friday was a repeat of discouraging weather, but we determined to have a go at it unless the weather should take a decided turn for the worse. We walked up the moraine, then climbed quickly, winding our way in and out of the clouds and following the cairns that would lead us to the col. At the col, we roped up. The path to the Rimpfischhorn lay to the right, but we turned left to tackle the Spitze Fluh, the peaklet (actually a gendarme) that marks the beginning of the Schwarz Grat. It was an amusing scramble up our first obstacle, with rotten rock and a fair amount of exposure. However, walking down the broad rocky ridge on the other side of the Spitze Fluh, I was reminded more of the Long Trail crossing Mount Mansfield or Boott Spur on Mount Washington than of the Alps.

From time to time the clouds parted, and one or another of the Zermatt giants revealed its snowy head. The heavy mist and fog produced an unusually heightened feeling of isolation, and though it wasn't what most would call a great day, there was a peace and serenity in the billowing clouds—a feeling of detachment from the world below and all its troubles. If sunny days are to be treasured, so, too, are stormy ones. Their beauty is no less compelling.

The big gendarme in the middle of the ridge proved to be the crux of the climb. It was quite steep, and until we found some telltale pitons and slings, we weren't altogether certain we were on the route. Even practice climbs have their *mauvais pas!*

The weather wasn't getting better, but the Fluhhorn —the end of the climb—was just ahead and it seemed reasonable to hope for a safe and dry return to Fluhalp and ultimately Zermatt. It was reasonable, but incorrect. All of a sudden, there was a strange buzzing sound that seemed to emanate from the rocks. We seemed to be in the center of this buzzing activity. In fact, we were!

Rony's hair literally stood on end just moments before the first burst of lightning and the almost simultaneous clap of thunder. Some readers may have experi-

enced electrical storms at high altitudes. For those of you
who haven't, let me assure you that they are far more
enjoyable to read about than to experience. Indeed, so
many Alpine narrations contain vivid accounts of these
sudden disturbances that I had developed a rather ho-
hum attitude about them. It can't happen here, thought I,
a veteran of ten seasons in the high mountains. "Local
thunderstorms" sound innocent enough when heard on
the radio in a chalet or mountain hotel, but on an exposed ridge at eleven thousand feet, they are an altogether
different matter!

The persistent crackling coming from Rony's sweater
convinced us that immediate retreat should be the order
of the day. Fortunately, we had but a short descent to
the final col before the Fluhhorn. We immediately headed
down a gully that must be easy under normal conditions.
However, the heavy snow forced us to exercise great care
on the loose and slippery rocks. Throughout our descent,
the lightning struck all around us and the thunder echoed
menacingly from cliff to cliff. By the time we were down,
the snow had changed to a driving rain. Far above, the
ridge was now totally white, covered by the fast-falling
snow. We were already soaked to the skin, so there was
no further discomfort as we marched along through the
pastures, boglike with the heavy rain. A couple of hot
grogs served by the kindly guardians at Fluhalp speeded
us on our way back to Zermatt.

More rain. Then, slowly improving weather, as we
began to have enough of village life. You don't have to
come all the way to Switzerland to haunt bars and drink
Irish coffee!

On the first clearing day—totally fogged in, but only
light rain—I decided to give my legs a good stretch. Up
to Riffelalp. Gornergrat was too far—more than five thousand feet above Zermatt—but what about Gagenhaupt,

that little promontory below the Riffelhorn? It was sup-
posed to be a popular meeting place for chamois and deer.
Alone, as I was, I fairly raced along the trail to Gagenhaupt, where, sure enough, I saw lots of the deerlike
creatures.

I took many photos, and a passing couple informed
me of the time. Only two hours to walk here! I decided
to push on to Gornergrat, and arrived in three hours—half
the signpost time! No doubt about it—fat was becoming
muscle and my lungs were working properly. An hour
and ten minutes of hard running and I was back in Zermatt. I was really in good form and spirits that day. I
went to Rony's to reserve his first free day for the Dom!

Then it was Thursday, August 27, and I found it
hard to believe that almost two weeks had passed. Lots
of fun, but no four-thousanders. This day, however, we
were on our way to the Dom Hut, and with a reasonable
weather forecast. Three and a half hours of uneventful
but steep ascent brought us to the hut, more than five
thousand feet above Randa. It was a perfect day, a refreshing breeze mitigating the heat of our effort, and
Rony setting a perfect pace. No puffing. In fact, not even
a drop of perspiration at our destination!

Evenings at huts are always a memorable experience
for me. I like the satisfaction after a hard walk up and the
special camaraderie that exists between fellow climbers
sharing a "home," if only for a matter of hours. I like the
dining-room reminiscences of earlier climbs. And there is
the breathtaking beauty of Alpine sunsets as the summits
turn gold, then pink, while the valley—seen dimly through
the haze—is a shadow far below. The gas lamps are lit,
pipes are smoked, provisions rearranged, and the Alpinist
clomps into the sleeping loft, usually before nine o'clock.

Sleep never comes easily. It's too early to "turn off"
and, besides, if you're like me, you're usually a little over-

Chamois near the Riffelhorn

stimulated at the prospect of the climb ahead. You are crowded into the *dortoirs*. Toss—turn—snort—an elbow from your neighbor—now he's got part of your blanket—oops, you have his! Cough—snore. Two thirty already!

Surely the human spirit ebbs at that time, New York bar experience to the contrary! Breakfast is always a force-feeding for me. Two bowls of tea and some stale bread, a last-minute check of gear, and Rony and I stumble out into the starry darkness.

First there's the inevitable half-blind groping over the loose rocks of the moraine, sputtering flashlights not quite getting the job done. But before long, the blood flows freely again and the sleep cobwebs fade away. We rope and strap on our crampons as we step onto the Festi Glacier. Only when we stop do I realize how penetrating the cold is. With gloves off, the steel crampons are icy against my hands.

We plod up over the glacier and then do some scrambling over the rock wall of the Festijoch. Six years earlier, this marked our high point, as apple juice and high winds put a stop to our plans for the Nadelgrat. Now, things are going well. A little tea, and we're off, descending several hundred feet down onto the Hohberg Glacier, skirting the tremendous *séracs* that fall from the Dom. Then up onto the steeper summit slopes—now at a height of over thirteen thousand feet.

For some strange reason, the steeper the slope becomes, the shorter my breath. Well, I always have this trouble the first day over thirteen thousand feet. Damn it! This is a lot of work. Why bother? Beach holidays must be nice. Or even picnics planned in the environs of the village. Is climbing Mount Everest really harder than this? Are those fellows human? My mind grumbles on.

Nine thirty: the summit. Such broad final slopes, and such a narrow crest for a summit ridge. Saas Fee is just beneath my left boot, the Täschhorn in front of my right one. I don't really feel like taking any pictures. Besides, it's too cold. However, I snap away: they'll make good souvenirs. Then down we go. Twenty minutes on top, after ten hours of very hard work. The ten hours are far more important than the twenty minutes as far as personal satisfaction goes.

Going down a steep snow slope is fun. The lungs are clear, the headache is gone, the scenery magnificent. Back on the Hohberg Glacier, it's blazingly hot now. Sun cream, frozen solid, has to be thawed. There's been a temperature change of fifty or sixty degrees in a couple of hours.

Back on the Festijoch, we found that those several hundred feet we had descended seemed much longer going back up—everything happened in reverse. Crampons off. Rope off. The hut—a change into warm clothes. Some hot soup. Total serenity. Back down the steep rocks. Raspberries and blueberries along the trail. Now we have time to eat them. Life, we decide in our exuberance, is a beautiful thing. Back in the village, we greet our friends with thumbs up!

The weather gods will smile now. My friend "sunny" Al Zesiger has arrived and he thinks Alpine storms are a rumor. He doesn't comprehend my limited accomplishments of the first two weeks. Saturday, we climb several thousand feet up the rocks above the train station. We run down the trail. The hard man is in great shape, ready to go. A freak of nature—rain—limits our exercise on Sunday to walking from one bar to another.

The weather cleared slowly. One day we hiked some of our favorite trails and did some practice climbing on the Tiefmatten rock. Al was having trouble lining up a guide for the Weisshorn. Zermatt guides have an increas-

ing predilection for the Matterhorn, an increasing abhor-
rence of leaving their village (Randa is half an hour
away) to do a climb. Special financial arrangements can
lure some of them, however, so we decided to go up to
the Matterhorn Hut and search out a "tiger" as Al's guide
for the Weisshorn. We almost ran up to the hut—an hour
and ten minutes for more than two thousand feet. At the
ten-thousand-foot level, it started to snow. "Sunny Al"
was beginning to understand! However, our mission was
successful. Al lined up a guide for Sunday and Monday
in case we couldn't make our mountain before the end
of the week.

Better weather! Wednesday morning at six A.M. we
were off for the famous "Hohenweg," considered by many
to be perhaps the most beautiful walk in Switzerland.
The walk is essentially flat, not more than a couple of
thousand feet of up and down, and runs south from
Hannigalp to the Alpine center of Saas Fee. Just a year
earlier, Al and I had started the Haute Route here.

Fortunately, clearing skies permitted us to witness
the spectacular views. First, to the north, the mighty
rock pyramid of the Bietschhorn thrust its black summit
through the clouds. In the foreground, the fir trees gave
the vista a Himalayan taste. Our first half hour was spent
eating blueberries, admiring the view, "peeling" for action. What followed was one of the most beautiful days
I have ever known. The path is a real mountain path,
rocky in places, narrow throughout, and enormously exposed in spots. There were places where we used our
hands to steady ourselves as we crept along in and out
of the buttresses dropping from the high peaks of the
Nadelgrat overhead. Brilliant sunlit views were succeeded
by ethereal cloud banks—reminding one of Japanese land-
scapes—which in turn gave way to sunshine once again.
The air was sweet, the fellow hikers we met along the

way were unvaryingly friendly. These moments make the
memories of a lifetime.

Far below, the Saas Valley unfolded—Saas Grund,
Saas Almagell, finally Saas Fee. Across from us rose the
Fletschhorn, Lagginhorn, and Weissmies, friends of earlier
summers. We had lunch in a blueberry patch, looking out
on a sparkling waterfall. Sausage, cheese, wine—everything tasted so good—and you don't have to pay for the
atmosphere, as you do in New York!

On Thursday, Al and I set out to climb the Cima di
Jazzi—the highest point (just under thirteen thousand
feet) between the Strahlhorn and the enormous east face
of Monte Rosa. But something is missing: a guide! Al
and I are recreational climbers of a highly amateur standard. Our knot-tying knowledge is incomplete, our rope-
handling abilities undeveloped. Our route-finding capa-
bilities are untested, our step-cutting technique untried.
Our courage is limited. We were well aware that this
climb was an adventure. True, the guidebook describes
our ascent as a "snow hike." But there were crevasses to
be avoided, and there was another guided party behind
us, so our form—or lack of it—would not go unnoticed!

The weather was beautiful. We could see our objective once we had topped the Stockhorn. It wasn't a big
climb by a long shot, but we made the most of it, enjoying every minute. An all-too-short two hours and fifteen
minutes and we were on top. The east face of Monte Rosa
dominated all, plunging down in a bold, seemingly vertical sweep into the mists that seethed up out of the
cauldron of the Val Anzasca and Macugnaga. The leg-
endary Marinelli Couloir faced us, an exacting and dangerous climb that claimed the life of the famous Zermatt
guide Alex Taugwalder—who tried to descend it. To my
knowledge no climber has accomplished this feat, but

the daredevil Valaisian Sylvain Saudan is reputed to have descended the death-dealing funnel on skis!

We spent an hour and a half on top, savoring the view, the sun, our friendship, our mountain experiences. Al and I realize our limitations and usually climb with guides. However, there was a certain joy in being on our own, in setting our own pace. Those of sterner stuff and more extensive training—those who always are on their own—will say "of course." To us, it was a revelation.

We still couldn't find a second guide for the Weisshorn, and since we were eager to make a climb together, we decided to return to the Theodul Hut and try Castor once more. Reports that the Weisshorn hadn't been climbed in several weeks—hence, no track—made our decision less painful than it might otherwise have been.

Back at the hut again, Al and I were excited at the prospect of climbing our first four-thousand-meter peak together. Friday, September 4, the last night that the hut would be open, the food was rather sparse. No matter, nothing short of bad weather could dampen our spirits. Fortunately, the stars were shining when we emerged after breakfast at four the next morning. It was very windy, but there were often high winds shortly before dawn.

We trudged up to the Breithorn Plateau. As we topped the slope that rises above Testa Grigia, we were hit by the full force of the wind, which we estimated to be fifty to sixty miles per hour. Winds of this force had turned us back on Mount Washington's Boott Spur the spring before, but then we were without the professional services of a Swiss guide. Behind Rony, we knew no fear.

We did know fatigue, however, as the biting wind chilled us to the bone. Al tried to take some motion pictures, but it was too cold to stand still for long. We

Fred Jacobson on the summit of Mont Pollux

traversed the breadth of the plateau, descended the Verra Glacier, and walked over to the base of the ridge rising to the summit of the Pollux, which Rony and I had climbed two years earlier. All this time we were climbing with another party bound for the Castor, under the leadership of René Arnold. As we approached the face of the peak, René was already hard at work, chopping steps up to the high-angle ice and snow bridge over a yawning crevasse.

Rony led, I followed, and Al brought up the rear. Rony had plenty of work, cutting additional steps and handholds as well as enlarging the steps from the other party. Communication was becoming an increasingly thorny problem, as the screaming wind made verbal exchanges nothing more than fragments. In the easier going, it didn't matter much. But on the belayed pitches, it raised havoc. Rony would lead off, with me belaying him from below. I would then climb up to him and in turn bring Al up on belay. The real problem was where the lead was so long that Al didn't have enough rope to pay out as I climbed. I then had to stop in midpitch, secure myself as best as I could, and wait for Al to join me before completing the pitch. We were on solid ice, the angle was more than forty-five degrees, and it was a distinct inconvenience to have lost verbal communication.

We waved each other on, or held up a temporizing hand. Ahead was a long exposed traverse of perhaps a hundred or even a hundred and fifty feet. Below, swirling mists concealed the empty space beneath our feet. The fatigue induced by our physical efforts was now heightened by nervous energy we were burning. And then—at the very crux—the mists rolled in, obscuring our visual communication. Even now, I shiver to think of that windswept and exposed corner. Tugs of the rope became our means of communication. And, since we had had no time for rehearsals, none of us knew what the others meant by the varying numbers of tugs.

In the heat of action, one is rarely philosophical. In the time since, I have looked back on those moments more than once. I remember being distinctly aware of the fact that a fall by any one of us would almost certainly have swept all three down the slope. However, I was honestly unafraid, too absorbed in surviving to worry much about whether or not I would survive.

The wind came in tremendous gusts, threatening to blow us right out of our steps. We dimly saw the silhouettes of the other party through the mists a few yards above us. As the ridge leveled out, and the summit loomed ahead of us, I experienced no elation, only a sudden dread of traversing that corner in descent. My thoughts were also with Al. This was only his second ice climb, and he surely was sharing my anxiety.

When we shook hands on the summit, we all felt the overwhelming emotion. Strong bonds are forged under stress. However, the challenge of the descent—that deadly corner, slippery and buffeted by the gale—prevented any lingering sentimentality.

Now it was time for the guides to show their mettle. They quietly explained the all-too-apparent dangers of descending the corner and told us we would rappell down the ice wall that the corner had skirted. Scylla and Charybdis! We all unroped, and the two ropes were tied together. Ice pickets were driven into the snow, and the ropes made fast to them. Rony threw the several hundred feet of rope over the wall, but the wind blew it straight out! So, grabbing it at the top and coiling it around his body, he let himself down into the swirling mists. We soon lost sight of him. Somehow, Rony conveyed his arrival at a platform. It was my turn. It wasn't a free rappell, but the wall was nearly vertical. Since there was no belay rope, it was hardly necessary for René Arnold to tell me not to let go! I arrived, kicked a few steps for myself and faced into the mountain, my nose virtually in the snow! One by one the party descended, each new arrival necessitating the "line" moving farther to the left—a precarious conga to say the least!

Finally, René climbed down around the corner. His effortless grace conveyed a technique I would never possess.

We roped again, and I led down through the still-dense clouds, straining for a trace of our earlier track. Once off the face of the Castor, we were in sunlight again, back in the world of the living. Lunch was our first stop in about seven hours. Our physical efforts plus the intense relief experienced after our escape combined to produce ravenous appetites. That night we all slept well.

Sunday, September 6. No climbing on Sundays. I was booked to return to New York from Geneva on Monday. Al had an extra day, so he left at noon for Randa and the Weisshorn Hut. I wished him the best, hoping he would be my proxy on the beautiful peak. My thoughts were with him the next day as the train took me down the valley past Randa. A week later I found out that Al had been on the summit at the very moment I had passed him, eleven thousand feet below.

Bad luck? I suppose. One more day of vacation and I would have shared the precious moments on the summit, this time sunlit and windless, but my days had been full, and my mountain had been courted—admittedly from a distance. I knew that one summer, all conditions would be right, and the white summit pyramid of the Weisshorn would feel the tread of my boots.

Chapter 12

New England Revisited

While the Alps were closest to my heart in the summer, more and more spring and autumn weekends were devoted to the mountains of New England. Having survived the rigors of our first nonskiing ski trip to Tuckerman's Ravine, we planned additional outings. In May of 1971, Charlie Walker, John McCabe, Al Zesiger, and I returned for another try. I had spent several weeks in bed with a pinched nerve in my neck. I was clearly not in top form, but we had planned this expedition for months, and I was determined not to miss it. We flew to Portland, Maine, and after a shore dinner drove over to Jackson. Sharing a cabin in the woods, we sat up late, sipping beers and planning our runs for the next day.

Al and Charlie went to bed and John opened up, sharing his anxiety about his forthcoming wedding. Old bachelors never die, they just fade away. In the middle of John's confessions, I abruptly excused myself with a splitting headache, something I almost never suffer. An hour later, I was returning the bad clam I had eaten at dinner. Violently ill for an hour, I finally fell asleep wondering whether the pinched nerve or general weakness would bother me more the next day!

The morning was so beautiful, however, that all my

pains and John's anxieties were forgotten. Lee, a girl I knew from New York, was to meet us at Pinkham Notch with three of her friends. We finally got together, organized our packs, skis, and frames, and set off up the Fire Trail. In incredibly short order, we were spread all over the mountain. Various subgroups waited for others who had already passed them via shortcuts. Yodels resounded, inevitably unanswered. Finally six of us were at the halfway point in the climb, at the base of the ravine. Since the laggards weren't skiing anyway, we set out up the ravine, arriving at the Lunch Rocks in good time. Here John put on a virtuoso display by greeting seemingly hundreds of skiers, all of whom were friends from Mad River. Since they offered to share their lunches with us, we offered the wine we were carrying (the laggards had our food).

Al set off for the summit with my friend Lee, while the rest of us settled down to the finest grapes the Rhine and Moselle could offer—Bernkasteler Doktor, Kröver Nacktarsch, Niersteiner, Domthal, Moselblümchen. We didn't see Al and Lee again until late in the day, a disappearing act that provided Charlie and John with countless opportunities to comment on the nature of Al's friendship. To this day, he assures me that the entire time was devoted to climbing and skiing. To this day, I guess I believe him.

John, Charlie, and I finally set off up the Headwall, stopping somewhat below the infamous Lip. Strapping on skis on a slope of forty-five degrees is an experience in itself. By the time we were ready to go, we were completely psyched out. We traversed for what seemed like miles and what in reality was probably five hundred feet. We finally made our first turns, pushing our skis through the fall line for a fleeting instant. A few sweeping turns and we were soon down—several hours of climbing for a couple of minutes of descent!

John joined me for another run, and then the three of

us watched Al and Lee come over the Lip, convinced by
their tentative slow-motion lurches that we had made a
wise choice not to test ourselves to that extent! We left our
skis in the woods, convinced that the weather would hold
for Sunday.

Our expectations were justified, and we were up early.
This time, we decided to ski Hillman's Highway—a narrow
gash that drops from Boott Spur, several hundred yards to
the left of the Headwall. The climb up is long and steep.
About two thirds of the way up, John decided to call it a
day. Above, the slope steepened and narrowed into the
Chimney. We could hardly admire the ever-widening
panorama that opened up below. At the top of Hillman's
Highway, we were almost four thousand vertical feet
above Pinkham Notch. At the top of Hillman's Highway,
Charlie Walker began to have some strange ideas. Obviously tired out by the long hike up, legs still aching from
yesterday's efforts, thoroughly intimidated by the drop off
through the Chimney (you couldn't see anything beneath
it), Charlie announced that he would not go down Hillman's Highway, but would traverse over to the summit
and ski down the easy Auto Toll Road. I pointed out that
the summit was several hours away and that since Al and
I had no intention of going there, it would be very dangerous for Charlie to go alone, particularly since the weather
was threatening to break. It was touch and go for half
an hour. It was also freezing for half an hour, since I had
given Charlie my parka to keep him warm. Finally, he
agreed to go down.

As on the Headwall, the first few turns were the
worst. You always think you will fall into space, but somehow you never do. We skied down through the Chimney,
where the slope widened and the angle eased off. There
we joined John and had a marvelous run down on perfect
spring snow—about fifteen to twenty minutes from top to

bottom. At the top of the run, we were well above timber-line, skiing in an Alpine world of rock and snow. At the bottom, we were weaving our way through the pine trees—a tremendously satisfying experience.

Spring skiing on Mount Washington presents several problems. Often, you have not been skiing for four or five weeks and you are not in top shape. The three- to four-thousand-foot-climb has sapped whatever strength you might have brought to the mountain. On top of that, your first run of the day is steeper than anything you've done all winter! Despite all of this, I think I enjoy this skiing more than any other, with the possible exception of the Haute Route in the Alps. We climbed halfway up Hillman's again and then skied down the steep but wide-open lower snowfields. Beautiful snow and a beautiful run. All too soon we were down. Driving back to Portland—and then to Boston, thanks to foul weather—we all agreed that an annual tradition had been established.

That autumn, we returned for a hiking weekend—Al, two of his sons, Dave Robison and two of his friends, John McCabe and I, as well as one girl, Kathy McCann, of Australia. Al, Dave, John, and I had all climbed in the Alps that summer, and Al's sons, Dave and Doug enjoyed the boundless energy that so often accompanies youth. Kathy and Dave's friends were the unknown quantities.

We started at a brisk pace, hiking through beautiful woods and crossing several streams along the way. For the first half hour, we followed the Fire Trail. Then we took a sharp right turn for Huntington Ravine. This is north of Tuckerman's, separated from it by Lion's Head and the Ravine of the Raymond Cataract. The turnoff is deliberately unmarked, as only very experienced hikers are expected to take this trail. Although it is considered a hike, a rope may be helpful for the less experienced mountain

John McCabe climbing the Huntington Ravine on Mount Washington

Al Zesiger and Dave Robison negotiating a slab at the
Huntington Ravine on Mount Washington

walkers, particularly if the rocks are wet. The trail is rocky, steep, and, in places where the slabs are fifty to sixty feet high, quite exposed.

Our group attacked with gusto. That is to say, most of us attacked. It was almost immediately apparent that Dave's friends were not up to our post-Alpine form! The telltale symptoms appeared: "Isn't that a lovely view?" "What is the name of this flower?" "Does that pinnacle over there have a route up it?" Finally the words were uttered: "Yes, we *are* tired." At one point, I had to climb back down to help one of them over a steep place.

At the top of Huntington Ravine, we turned left to the summit. Despite the long waits for the exhausted climbers, we had still been less than three hours to the top. It was only eleven and hardly time to turn down. We quickly decided to head north, aiming first for Mount Clay. On its summit, we decided to split up. Dave's friends would go back, well satisfied with having climbed two peaks in one day. John McCabe would see them safely down. The remaining six of us would keep going.

From Mount Washington, the so-called northern peaks include Clay, Jefferson, Adams, and Madison. Why not try to do all of them? The ridge was broad and rocky —lovely Alpine rambling—it never dropped below five thousand feet—and we were all fit. After a brief lunch, we set out.

The weather was not promising. Earlier it had been somewhat cloudy. Now the clouds pretty much blotted out whatever panorama there might have been. As a result, there wasn't much temptation to stop and admire the view. The climb up Jefferson was considerably longer than the climb up Clay, and it was at this point that we began to doubt the sanity of our program! Whenever we met a party coming from the other direction, they first congratulated us on having gotten that far and then assured us that we could get no farther and still return by dark.

Although none of us knew the area well, we smiled good-naturedly (perhaps somewhat smugly) at their lack of confidence. Nevertheless, as we got a view of Adams—the highest of the White Mountains after Mount Washington—it did seem quite far away. We plodded on and on—that evening, a number of us admitted to intermittent muscle cramps—winding our way over boulder fields, the hiking never difficult, but demanding constant attention.

The weather was not getting better, and time was running out. Finally, about ten minutes below the summit of Adams, we took a bypass trail that led directly to the Madison Huts. They were closed, but a number of campers assured us we would not get back to Pinkham by dark. My guidebook suggested three and a half hours for the return, but I knew better. It was less than four thousand feet down, and we would probably take half that time. But the campers—experienced hikers in the area—assured us it was a long, long way. It was now four thirty and we should start immediately. We could not count on daylight much past six o'clock.

The Madison Gulf Trail is one of the most rugged I have ever hiked, seemingly a dried-up streambed. The descent is steep, over large boulders and almost continuously awkward. Anything more difficult would require a rope. We'd been on the go for about nine hours and our legs felt it. We were involved in a race with the sun. Although we got down the most difficult part, the sun was easily the winner. Just below the Great Gulf Shelters, where more sensible people were settling down for the night, the darkness set in. Only Al and I had our flashlights. I led and he brought up the rear, while the others struggled in between the lights.

No one complained as we groped down the Great Gulf and Osgood trails. The trails were very difficult to follow, since leaves covered the ground and gave the terrain a confusing sameness. From time to time, Kathy would embrace a tree, the only sign of her complete exhaustion. The rest of us limped along quietly. Once we lost the trail, and it seemed we were fated to pass the night in the woods. After fifteen suspenseful minutes, we were back on track. When we finally saw headlights in the near distance, we couldn't believe we were almost out of it. We doubled our caution, as even there a turned ankle could have had serious implications! At seven forty-five, just twelve hours after starting, we stepped out of the woods!

Our margin of safety had been rather precarious. As leader, I felt responsible for miscalculating the time required for the descent. By the time dinner was over, however, all of us felt it had been one of our greatest days in the mountains.

In 1972, we returned to Tuckerman's once more for spring skiing. This time we planned two trips—one at the end of April and one near the end of May. In April we were able to ski all the way down to Pinkham Notch, a four-thousand-foot descent, reasonably long even by Alpine standards. The weather was clear and the panorama from the top of Hillman's was unforgettable. Close by, there was a narrow chute of rock and snow. Farther back, we faced the awesome steepness of the Headwall. The valley was at our feet, while the mountain ranges surrounded us, extending as far as we could see. The second day, we went to Wildcat, enjoying another perfect day and the lazy delights of skiing with the aid of lifts!

In May, we drove up the Toll Road, sunning near the summit rocks and skiing the very steep but wide-open summit snowfields on the final cone itself. Then we made a beautiful Alpine traverse over to the Headwall and had a breathtaking run down the Left Gully, surely the steepest and narrowest run I have taken or ever will take. One year we will take a week and explore more fully the limitless possibilities of spring skiing on Mount Washington!

Chapter 13

How Not to Enjoy the Alps

The summer of 1971 was unusual in that I didn't climb with Rony. Because of illness, he was out for the season. Al had climbed the Weisshorn the previous summer with a man from Täsch. And that winter I had skied one day with this fellow's brother, who was also a mountain guide.

As the summer approached, Al and I discussed possible climbs. Judging from past experiences, we felt the only way to do what we wanted was to hire a pair of guides for an "engagement." This way, for two weeks, they would climb with us exclusively, wherever and whenever we chose. Otherwise, we were afraid that no one would go with us to the more distant areas. We decided to try the men from Täsch, and each of us wrote a letter to the one we knew. No response to a total of four letters. Finally, we sent a yes-no checklist with self-addressed stamped envelopes. About a week before our departure, we finally got replies in the affirmative.

We made several mistakes at the outset. The first was financial. The normal arrangement, per the tariff book, is to pay the guide 120 Swiss francs per day plus thirty percent of the normal tariff for each peak climbed. We assumed this was the only arrangement and so neglected to come to a firm agreement ahead of time. This neglect was to lead to considerable unpleasantness at the premature end of our engagement.

The second mistake was to hire the guides for a period starting immediately after our arrival in Zermatt. Against my better judgment, Al had persuaded me to do this, reasoning that the weather would be bad at least half of the time and that it would be wise to have our men for as many good days as possible. Thanks to increasingly rigorous training, I had gotten away from my earlier practice of doing no climbing the first week, using the time to walk and acclimatize. Nevertheless, arriving on a Friday night and heading for a hut on Sunday is pushing it a bit.

We decided to go to the Bordier Hut, far above St. Niklaus. From there we would climb the Balfrin and Gross Bigerhorn one day and then start at the Dürrenhorn and see how far we could get on the Nadelgrat the second day. Our trip to the hut—or, rather, to St. Niklaus—was an omen of things to come! Al and I were to meet Peter (a pseudonym), who was climbing the Matterhorn, at the one o'clock train in Zermatt, pick up Fritz (another pseudonym) in Täsch, and then proceed to St. Niklaus, where we would take a taxi to Ried and then walk to the hut. That was the plan; it didn't work. Not only was Peter not at the station, but Al was also late. There were two trains five minutes apart, so when Al didn't appear I decided to wait for him and take the second one. Still no Al, so I got on the second train, only to discover that it didn't stop in Täsch, but only in Randa. And it didn't go as far as St. Niklaus.

Trying to keep my cool, I chose to jump off the train at Täsch and look for Fritz, who must have been disappointed and confused by the three-sided "no-show." A few inquiries convinced me that Fritz had stuck to the

original plan and taken the earlier train. I was now on
my own and rather confused myself. I hitched to St.
Niklaus, and on arrival at the station, I saw Al paying a
taxi driver! Well, at least we were there, more or less on
time. Fritz was waiting at the station, quite unruffled.
However, there was no trace of Peter. Evidently, his client
hadn't been as speedy as he had hoped on the Matterhorn, so we could do nothing but wait for him.

Finally Peter arrived; a taxi was immediately ordered;
and we set off for the hut. The guidebook suggested three
and a half to four hours as the average time for the walk.
We set off at what was for Al and me a rather breathless
pace. When I developed some blisters—not unusual for
the first forced march—things became quite clear. The
guides didn't stop, but kept going at their own pace. Once
I had put some padding on the sore spots, I pushed hard
to catch up with the others, and finally caught up at the
edge of the Ried Glacier. Here it was Al's turn to fall
back. He had a little trouble avoiding slips on the ice,
merely from lack of experience. Fritz—Al's guide—walked
away in disgust, ignoring his struggling pupil. Finally,
Peter was kind enough to show Al the proper way, and he
had no more problems. We arrived at the hut in just three
hours, an hour less than the recommended time. My
guide's comment was: "Hmph, that was like a funeral pro-
cession!"

The handwriting was on the wall, but neither of us
wanted to read it. The next day we set off at about five
o'clock for the Balfrin. Guidebook time was three and a
half hours. It was an easy climb—some light crevasse work
on a relatively flat glacier and scrambling on a rocky ridge.
At a little past seven thirty, we were on top. Our guides
again commented that we would have to go faster. We
were back at the hut well before lunch time, satisfied with

our first day—a climb to 3800 meters—despite the rather unkind comments of our guides.

After lunch, there was a thunderstorm, but we were sure it would quickly clear off. It did that day, but when we arose at two for the Dürrenhorn, we were completely fogged in. At four, the situation was no better, nor at six. Finally, at seven thirty, it cleared, but by then it was too late to start out.

After breakfast, then, we returned to Zermatt. The next day, Wednesday, I decided to practice rock climbing on the Riffelhorn, while Al traversed the Leiterspitzen— a difficult rock ridge that I had climbed back in 1960, with Benny Perren. We planned to meet at the Täsch Hut and make plans for climbs from there.

The Riffelhorn was a disaster! After twelve years of happily albeit clumsily roaming about its rocks, I was brought short by Peter's constant flow of insults. Since I was a rather marginal rock climber to start with, what little confidence I brought to my first day of serious climbing was soon shattered! At one point, my little friend (he is almost a foot shorter than I am, though far stronger) threatened to pull me off the rocks with the rope if I didn't perform more elegantly. At that point I hated him. I had never realized climbing could be so little fun.

Back in the village, a phone message said Al would be back in town; we would go to the Täsch Hut the following evening, instead. When I saw Al, he spoke enthusiastically of the Leiterspitzen, but something seemed to be missing; I was not convinced! A day of rain gave us a brief reprieve, but late on Friday afternoon, we left Zermatt by taxi for Täschalp and then the hut.

More writing on the wall—the taxi ran out of gas less than halfway to Täschalp. Ordinarily, this would be no problem, since the walk is a simple one. However, we had

Clouds boil over the frontier ridge above Zermatt

The Matterhorn rising above Zermatt

left late enough so that we would now probably arrive after dark. On top of that, it was raining and the sky was heavy all around us. In desperation, we phoned the hut from Täschalp, hoping that our guides would not be there or would tell us to go on down because of the weather. No such luck. Our Simon Legrees merely told us to hurry up!

We arrived at the hut at about eight o'clock and were immediately cheered by the sight of two rather attractive Dutch girls who were hiking from hut to hut through the Valais. All too soon, it was nine thirty, past bedtime. We had three alternatives: if the weather was excellent, we would get up at one o'clock to try the traverse of the Täschhorn and Dom; if it were only fair, we would get up two hours later and climb the Alphubel; if the weather remained bad, we could have a good sleep and return to Zermatt!

Having looked forward to climbing all year, I now found myself praying for bad weather, much comforted by the wind that howled around the hut. I imagined the loathsome Peter hurling threats at the weather gods above the gale. And I smiled in satisfactions as they hurled them back.

The next thing I knew, my tormentor was standing in front of me shouting in an earsplitting whisper that it was time to get up. As I sleepily dressed I couldn't imagine setting out for the Alphubel in such marginal weather. Groping in the dark, I stumbled downstairs and asked the hutkeeper what time it was. Ten minutes to one! We would try the Täschhorn–Dom after all! It was Saturday, August 7—my birthday—and it would be a long one! We left the hut at two, in full moonlight. There was a strong wind, but the sky seemed clear. Around us, everything was bathed in a silver light, but there was no time to admire the breathtaking scenery. Our men set off at a good clip, and there was no time for such distractions as enjoying yourself!

We contoured some grassy slopes, crossed a large boulder field and moraine, and set off up the Weingarten Glacier. It would have been nice to have had crampons on, but our men felt that this would have involved an unnecessary delay. They urged us to pick up the pace. We heartily endorsed the idea, but our legs and lungs limited us. We tried to communicate this shortcoming to our disgruntled partners.

The details of the climb are really unimportant. Suffice it to say that the Täschhorn is reputed to be the least-climbed peak in the Zermatt area. And for good reason. All of its ridges, including the Mischabelgrat, which we climbed, are composed of loose rock. The dangers are constant. As we rose higher, clouds set in, and before long the driving wind contained snowflakes. To give our guides their due, not many would have made the peak that day. In retrospect, I'm not sure it was worth it. Well along the ridge I fell some five minutes behind Al and Fritz. Peter, furious at this turn of events, gave a fierce tug on the rope. I have a scar from the sharp rock my leg struck in response to Peter's gentle tug. After all of this abuse, we were on our peak in seven hours, half an hour faster than recommended time!

We assumed we would traverse the peak, descending the snow face that leads eventually to the Dom Hut. It is considered to be the fastest route off the mountain. But our men had other ideas—we would go back the way we'd come. Barely concealing our disappointment, we headed back down the lengthy ridge. It was too much for our first four-thousand-meter climb that summer. Al and I were both very tired on the way down. Our guides' expressions of sympathy were limited to further insults, including recommendations as to what exercises we use for

training. I suggested that perhaps the Mischabelgrat on
the Täschhorn was not the ideal location for mapping out
a physical-fitness plan! By three thirty we were back in
Täschalp. We had climbed a great mountain, but we were
far from elated. That night at dinner—my friend Norbert
had arrived and joined us—we concentrated our thoughts
on the mountain and tried to forget the guides.

However, the next day, Sunday, Al told me he would
go home on Tuesday, a week early. He found it less than
fun to be treated as we had been, and I could hardly
disagree. On Monday we hiked up the Mettelhorn—six
thousand feet above Zermatt—with our new Dutch friends.
The day was beautiful, the company delightful, and the
view from the top extraordinary. While the Mettelhorn is
essentially a hike, you must cross a snowfield and scramble
up some fairly steep rocks at the summit. You definitely
feel as though you're on a mountain peak. And the
panorama is, in my opinion, the finest in the Zermatt area.
We sunned on the summit rocks for a couple of hours,
looking alternately at the Weisshorn, which Al had
climbed a year earlier, and the Täschhorn, our "conquest"
of two days ago. On the way down, we stopped often—to
pick flowers, to finish our picnic, to admire the view, to
savor every minute of a beautiful day.

The next day, Al left. I terminated the engagements
with the guides, who were quite unhappy not to be paid
for the second week and had expected 150 francs per day
for their efforts, despite the 120-franc tariff listed. I made
several long hikes with Norbert, and returned home a
week later. The following summer was to be quite different!

Chapter 14

The Man-Eater

After years of deliberation, I finally decided to take a three-and-a-half-month leave of absence from my job to write a book about climbing. As my departure date of June 13 approached, I found it hard to believe that I would be temporarily unemployed. My first goal was, of course, to write this book. Second, but equally important, I wanted to finish those "four thousanders." With a whole summer to get in shape, the long climbs should be within my powers, more so than during a two- or three-week holiday, at the end of which I am usually just starting to get into top shape.

With farewell parties and the extra effort required at the office to leave things in reasonable order, there was practically no time for running. I didn't mind the fact that I was a little out of shape and somewhat overweight; a few weeks of hiking would take care of that. I did regret that I had not built up my mental toughness through the discipline of daily running. However, that would come too.

Somehow, the weather in Zermatt is usually "unusual." The spring of 1972 was unusually late, and the snow was much lower than most years in the middle of June. It was immediately apparent that the climbing season would not

start before mid-July, at least two weeks behind schedule.
I had brought my skis over, thinking that I might put in
a few days between writing, climbing, and hiking. As
things turned out, I got a season's pass and skied almost
every day in June. The weather was generally warm and
sunny, and I had great fun skiing with the staff of the
European Camp Association—mostly Americans, with a
liberal sprinkling of Swiss, Scots, and Dutch. When we
were on the glacier (it was still safe to go off the piste *),
our greatest pleasure was to carve turns in the fresh light
powder. The skiing was so good that it was easy to wait
patiently for the start of the climbing.

Rony and I met several times to discuss our activities
for the summer. As always, we would warm up on the
Riffelhorn. And then, there were the last of the "four
thousanders." The climbs remaining were the long-coveted
Weisshorn, the Dent d'Hérens, the fearsome Lyskamm,
and finally the Nadelgrat, first tried eight long years ago.
These peaks were all well known to me. They are all long
climbs, all among the more difficult climbs that Zermatt
has to offer. With a whole summer to acclimatize and get
into shape, Rony and I were confident that we could do
them.

The snows lingered, and it was July 14, exactly a
month after arrival when Rony and I finally devoted
part of a day to the Riffelhorn. It was a particular pleasure
to be on the rope again with my good friend, especially
after the problems of the previous summer. The steep
rocks were warm to the touch and I felt a great exhilaration
and joy. This marked the beginning of the tenth year of
my partnership with Rony, and it was to be a memorable
season.

---

* Those portions of the glaciers or snowfields which are generally
packed are called pistes.

July 19. The Gornergrat train after a day of skiing? Yes, the next day was slated for our assault on the Lyskamm, the huge double-peaked mountain so Himalayan in character, whose German nickname meant "Man-Eater." The name is derived from the fact that the knife-edge snow-and-ice ridge connecting the two summits often has cornices, sometimes double cornices, which in the past have swept parties to their deaths when they detached themselves from the main ridge.

As I walked from the Rotenboden Station across the Gorner Glacier to the Monte Rosa Hut, with the Lyskamm towering directly over me, I couldn't help wondering about those cornices. Would the Man-Eater be hungry tomorrow?

I arrived at the hut and met Rony, who had climbed the Monte Rosa that day. It seemed that the Lyskamm had been climbed once that summer, a week earlier, but the tracks had been totally covered by fresh snow. No parties had attempted the peak after the heavy snowfalls.

There are two ways to approach the traverse of the Lyskamm. The usual way is to set out from the Monte Rosa Hut, climb several of the summits of Monte Rosa, and sleep at the Capanna Margherita, the little hut perched on the summit of the Signalkuppe at close to fifteen thousand feet, the highest hut in the Alps. The advantage is obvious: by sleeping at such a great altitude, you avoid the tiring five- to six-hour climb up the Grenz Glacier to the Lysjoch before tackling the ridge of the Lyskamm. Theoretically, you are fresher and better able to enjoy the actual climbing.

However, the advantage is more theoretical than actual, since few people are able to sleep at all, let alone well, in the lofty hut. Therefore, after a sleepless night, the average climber sets out with a headache. The second problem with this approach is that if the weather changes while you are at the Margherita Hut, it is not easy to get down from this great height.

The other way to traverse the Lyskamm is directly from the Monte Rosa Hut. This makes it a long climb—thirteen to fourteen hours—but it has the advantage of getting you up and down the peak in a single day. The mountain is usually traversed from east to west—from the Lysjoch to the Feliksjoch—and the entire ridge is well over four thousand meters. For several hours, you are higher than the Matterhorn. From the Feliksjoch, it is possible to return to the Monte Rosa Hut by the Zwillings Glacier, but this is extremely dangerous and most parties avoid this route. You can either descend to the Quintino Sella Hut in Italy and then return to Zermatt over the Castor and across the Breithorn Plateau the next day or you can try to do it all in a single day. The complete traverse is better done from the Margherita Hut.

Rony and I wanted to do the direct route and planned to spend the night at the Sella Hut. We went to bed early, leaving a call in for two o'clock. The call was hardly necessary, as I never fell asleep, thanks to somewhat less than ideal sleeping conditions. The mattresses at Swiss Alpine Club huts are one half the normal size at best, and on this crowded evening, there were three climbers for every two mattresses. "Love thy neighbor?"

We were among the first up. Several parties were planning to do the traverse of Monte Rosa, but we were to be alone on the Lyskamm. Rony had done the climb several times before, but never directly from the Monte Rosa Hut. Ideally, we would have liked a track and some company on the climb. We left the hut at three and for several hours walked up moraines and then easy glacier terrain. Those bound for the Dufourspitze turned left, as we continued on up the Grenz Glacier. This early in the season, it was quite straightforward. Later in the summer, route-finding would become a distinct problem, as the glacier moved and new crevasses opened.

There were a number of other roped parties threading their way through the crevasses. Ideally, it is best to have at least three on a rope for glacier work. To offset the fact that we were only two, Rony and I were attached by a double rope—one tied round my waist and the other through my chest sling. At close to four thousand meters, we separated from those who were traversing the Monte Rosa from the Signalkuppe, heading more to the right— on untracked snow—for the Lysjoch, the point of departure for our traverse.

The snow was solid, holding our weight most of the

Monte Rosa, queen of the Alps

time. Nevertheless, at the Lysjoch (its altitude of 4250 meters is higher than most of the Zermatt peaks!), I felt quite ill. They were the usual altitude complaints—headache, nausea, fatigue. Furthermore, the awesome aspect of the undulating razor-sharp ridge now in full view made me doubt my ability to go on. It was a big expedition for our first outing, and the weather seemed to be changing, dark clouds brewing on the Italian side of Monte Rosa. These are the pivotal times in any big climb.

After a fifteen-minute halt, I felt somewhat better, and Rony and I decided to give it a good try. This was by far the biggest climb Rony had attempted since his illness the previous summer, and the absence of tracks on our solitary traverse must have raised doubts in his own mind. But whatever he may have felt, I heard only words of encouragement.

The first part of the ridge to the east peak went well enough, not too steep and not too exposed. The snow was excellent, and no steps were required. As we neared the final slopes of the east peak, however, the snow suddenly got very soft. We sank in as far as our knees, tiring work on a forty- to forty-five-degree slope at a height of almost fifteen thousand feet. Rony had the hardest job, breaking the track. Since I am about thirty pounds heavier, I sank in still farther. Two hours from the Lysjoch, we were on top of the fourth highest peak in Europe!

We halted briefly, enjoying a rather limited view, since the clouds obscured much of the surroundings. No questions were asked; of course we would complete the traverse.

Between the east and west peaks of the Lyskamm runs one of the sharpest ridges I have ever crossed. It must vary in character from year to year, perhaps from week to week. When we crossed it, it was rarely more than a foot wide, more often a matter of a couple of

The north face of the Lyskamm from the top of the Grenz Glacier with the Dent d'Hérens and the Matterhorn in the background

inches. There was almost no ice, which meant that we could move on the snow together almost throughout. On either side, walls of forty to fifty-five degrees dropped off for several thousand feet or more. While the absence of a track meant more work for us, it was a far more beautiful experience to cross the virgin snows, leaving our own imprint on the ridge. We were alone in a vast world of ice and snow, of dizzying precipices, of delicate and airy snow ridges, of gigantic *séracs* and hanging glaciers. At the end of the climb, Rony exclaimed, "We can thank God for this day," and I had to agree.

The climb between the two peaks went smoothly, lasting about two and a half hours. Just before the west

peak, some rocks broke up the ridge. This mixed terrain
of rock and snow was the most delicate part of the climb.
The exposure was extreme, so much so that I couldn't take
it seriously and maintain my powers of locomotion. One
cannot slip in such a place. It is here that guide and client
must have perfect trust in each other.

And then the airy tightrope walk was over. We were
on the west peak. Mallory's words reechoed in my mind—
"What have we conquered? Have we vanquished an
enemy? Naught but ourselves." I was supremely grateful
to have been permitted to pass several hours on this in-
finitesimally small part of our earth. Measured against it,
we were equally infinitesimal. Measured against ourselves
eleven hours earlier, we had grown considerably.

The Dent d'Hérens seen from the Schönbühl Hut

One of my regrets in high-altitude climbing is that there is never adequate time to indulge in meditation and fully appreciate the wondrous scenery in which you find yourself. All too soon, we had to leave the summit, heading down to the Sella Hut or back to the Monte Rosa Hut.

But a quick change in the weather made the descent far more than we had bargained for. Suddenly it became unbearably hot, the sun burning right through our shirts. The fog and haze seemed to magnify its intensity. One moment there had been some snow flurries; now there was scorching, searing heat. Aside from creating personal discomfort, it had a disastrous effect on the snow, which, with the exception of the final slopes on the east peak, had been excellent. Now it was completely rotten. We sank in to our knees. I was leading down, and the snow balled up under my crampons, making it difficult to take a step without sliding around helplessly. Rony quickly suggested we remove our crampons, which provided some relief. Nevertheless, we had a struggle getting down to the Feliksjoch over terrain that was considerably easier than we had already climbed. Arriving at the pass, we had three alternatives.

To the right lay the Zwillings Glacier, reported to be the most treacherous in Zermatt. With no track, dangerously soft snow, and two on a rope alone in the late afternoon, this clearly wasn't a feasible alternative!

Straight ahead lay Castor, little more than an hour's climb to its summit. But, the opposite face could be dangerously avalanche-prone. And the Verra Glacier, which leads to the Breithorn Plateau and relative safety, would make hard going with obviously rotten snow. The lure of the nearest shelter was too much for both of us, and we turned left, aiming for the Sella Hut, out of sight some four hundred meters below us.

What should have been a half hour's gambol stretched

into an hour and a half of exhausting hiking over snow that often collapsed under us. I had had more than enough and gave out a fairly steady stream of unprintables as I sank in, often above my knees. We moved automatically, plodding dully over the endless snowfields. We finally spotted the hut and made our way painfully to its door. There were eight other climbers who had come up that day from Italy. Five of them were from my hometown—Scarsdale, New York. Suburbia seemed far away to all of us! Shortly after we arrived at the hut, a heavy snowstorm broke. But it didn't matter; the Man-Eater had been kind to us.

Friday it was clear, and we were on top of the Castor in little more than two hours, a beautiful *promenade* after the trials of the preceding day. Avalanche tracks on the other side convinced us of our wisdom in avoiding it the day before. We descended quickly on good snow.

We crossed the Verra Glacier under a scorching sun, sinking hip deep in the slushy snow as we fought our way toward the Breithorn Plateau and the route to Zermatt.

The snow finally firmed up as we were descending the slopes above the Plateau Rosa. Friends were shooting by on skis, their questions answered by thumbs up, as I had momentarily lost my voice. We virtually ran down to Trockener Steg, then caught the cable car down to Zermatt.

It was Rony's and my biggest climb together, and it had come off without a hitch. It was a favorable omen of bigger and even better things to come.

Chapter 15

A Most Difficult "Tooth"

The Dent d'Hérens was next on our program. I had looked on it with awe for the last five years, and my respect for the massive peak was sharpened by the guidebook, which described it as technically the most difficult four-thousand-meter peak in the Zermatt area, perhaps in all the Alps. This referred to the normal route. Many mountains have very difficult special routes, such as, for example, the north faces of the Eiger and the Matterhorn. But most of these mountains, including the two named above, have relatively easy normal routes. What sets the Dent (tooth) apart is that there is no truly easy way up it. The least difficult route is described as *assez difficile*—difficult enough.

On Monday, July 24, Rony and I met at Stafelalp, the little mountain inn perched on a slope beneath the north face of the Matterhorn. Rony had traversed the Wellenkuppe and Obergabelhorn that day, and we were to set out for the Schönbühl Hut that evening and tackle the Dent d'Hérens. Originally, Rony had felt that we should attack the peak (which he had never climbed) only in tandem with another guided party. However, our performance on the Lyskamm had added to his confidence in us as a team, and now he was prepared to go it alone.

The weather, however, was unstable on the twenty-fourth. We had a consultation and decided we shouldn't chance it.

On July 30, we were back at Stafelalp. Once again, the skies were threatening, but this time the weather report was encouraging. Realizing that one must always risk something on the bigger climbs, we set out for Schönbühl. During the two-hour hut walk, it rained, hailed, and finally snowed. However, once we had made our decision, we wouldn't turn back unless the weather turned bad on the climb itself. Needless to say, we were soaked by the time we reached Schönbühl. In a typically correct but unfriendly gesture, the hutkeeper's wife would not let us dry out our shirts in the kitchen. There were only eight climbers in the hut. It would have created no problems, but rules were rules. Most hutkeepers are old mountain guides, true lovers of the mountains and mountain climbers. At Schönbühl, however, the hutkeeper and his wife remained aloof from the climbers; they seemed to be earning their living and no more.

We were up at one o'clock for breakfast, along with another party attempting the Zmutt Ridge of the Matterhorn. For the first time in all my climbing years, the hutkeepers were not even up. They had left everything on the tables, including tea in a Thermos! The weather was totally "socked in," with clouds obscuring all of the surrounding peaks. Nevertheless, we set out, determined at least to reconnoiter our mountain and, if the weather cleared up, to try for the top.

The Dent d'Hérens is far away from the Schönbühl Hut. To get to it, you must descend a moraine, cross the Schönbühl Glacier, traverse the moraine of the Stockje Glacier, and then climb up the lower and upper ice falls of the notoriously difficult and dangerous Tiefmatten Glacier. All of this, just to get to the base of the actual climb!

The Haute Route—two views of the west face of the
Matterhorn from near Schönbühl

There were no problems at the outset—down the moraine and across the Schönbühl Glacier. On the Stockje Moraine, we lost our way several times, stumbling around in the endless blocks of rubble, rising and dropping down, searching for a way on to the Tiefmatten Glacier. When we found it, it lived up to its reputation. A comment in the hut book had spoken of "criminal snow bridges" over some of the crevasses, and we soon found out what they meant. In places, we almost had to crawl over them. There was already a track from one of the three other parties who had climbed the mountain that year, and that saved us at least a couple of hours of complicated route-finding. We wound around, over, and even through some giant *séracs;* these enormous blocks of ice were very precariously balanced. Several times it looked as though we wouldn't get through at all. In places, gigantic crevasses stretched across almost the entire glacier, necessitating wide and time-consuming detours.

Slowly but surely we mounted into a wild and lovely mountain cirque. On our right was the Col de Valpelline— our Haute Route pass of three years ago—and the Tête de Valpelline. Straight ahead of us were avalanche-swept slopes leading up to the depression in the ridge known as the Tiefmattenjoch. And on our left was the Dent d'Hérens!

We would ascend the northwest flank, actually another glacier, squeezed in between two precipitous ridges. When we finally reached the foot of the face, where we made our only rest stop of the ascent, it was six thirty. It had taken us four and a half hours to get to our climb. Now we were alone amid some of the most savage mountain scenery I have ever seen.

The face itself is only some seven hundred meters— less than twenty-five hundred feet. But it is real climbing, the lower half of the face having an average inclination of forty-eight degrees (compared to the Hörnli Route on the Matterhorn, which is thirty-nine degrees). The difficulties began almost immediately, and we put on our crampons. A short steep snow slope led up to the bergschrund, the giant crevasse that spans the entire face. In some years, the mountain cannot be climbed because it is impossible to pass this overhanging crack (the upper lip protrudes over the lower one).

We had some ice screws with us, and these were quickly brought into action as we hammered them in and hauled ourselves up and over the blue depths of the bergschrund. Above it, a snow slope of not less than sixty degrees led through the giant *séracs* that covered the face.

Col de Fenêtre

This was the steepest snow climbing I had ever done. Roughly paralleling the "three points of contact at all times" doctrine of rock climbing, we first inserted the ice ax and then pressed in with the front points of our crampons.

The snow was perfect, and once I had made the psychological adjustment to this vertical white world, progress was quite rapid. When Rony saw that I was comfortable, we moved simultaneously almost throughout the climb. As we mounted, I wondered how I would ever be able to climb down this dizzying slope. After the steepest pitches, the face would level off. We were mounting a series of risers—a gigantic staircase. There were two more large crevasses to deal with, but ice screws and tubes* made short order of these difficulties. The upper half of the face eases off to a far more reasonable thirty-five-degree snowfield. It is somewhat longer than it looks and is capped off with a rock ridge, offering interesting scrambling at an altitude of thirteen thousand feet. We worked our way along the ridge until suddenly there was nothing but clouds at our feet. In fact, only the summit of the Matterhorn pierced the impenetrable cloudbank engulfing the Pennine Alps that day.

There were tears of joy in my eyes. It was an emotional moment, standing on top of this most difficult peak. The climb of the face itself had taken only three hours, but it was a time of intense concentration and all-out effort. On the summit, my only regret was that my friend Al could not be there. We had dreamed of the peak together, admired it on the Haute Route, and discussed how we might best approach it. He had not been able to get away this summer, and my thoughts were with him as I stood on the pointed peak.

* Hollow screws which hold particularly well in hard snow.

But it was too cold to linger long, and the continuously threatening weather made it imperative to head down without delay. The rocks required some care, and then we were able to move swiftly down the upper snowfield. A brief halt, and then we started down the ice fall. I faced inward and found that the holes made by our ice axes on the way up served as excellent fingerholds. I drove in my ice ax with one hand, and inserted two fingers from the other in the existing holes and pressed in the front points of my crampons. This technique worked wonderfully well, and our progress was halted only by the three giant crevasses, which did cause some difficulty. The last one had to be jumped, a feat that left my heart in my throat!

Once below this last difficulty, I suggested that we pause for tea. Almost before Rony could respond, two stones the size of baseballs plummeted by my head. We were in the line of the mountain's artillery, and clearly this was not the place to stop if we valued our lives. Throughout the descent, I had a strange presentiment that the mountain resented our intrusion and would do everything possible to complicate our escape. This attack heightened my feelings. And, a couple of hours later, when we discovered that several of the snow bridges we had crossed earlier were now collapsed under the day's heat, I once again felt the mountain's "presence."

We were back at Stafelalp some fourteen hours after we had set out from Schönbühl. While the weather had been a cause for concern, the snow had been uniformly excellent. Rony and I had added a new mountain to our collection, and for me, only two climbs remained and my dream would be realized!

Chapter 16

The Weisshorn and the Last "Four Thousander"

Sunday, August 6, was the eve of my thirty-fourth birthday. Exactly a year ago I had set out for the Täschhorn. Now Rony and I were boarding the train once again for Randa, this time to walk up to the Weisshorn Hut! We had courted the mountain long enough; now the time was ripe, and we were going to attempt the peak the following day.

We took a late train to Randa, because Rony had climbed on the Riffelhorn that day and his family had joined him for a picnic at the foot of the rocky peak. I became increasingly anxious as two fifty-three—departure time—approached on the station clock. No Rony! In fact, he didn't show up until two fifty-six, but by a stroke of good luck, a Swiss train actually departed four minutes late. We found a door open and jumped on as the train started in motion!

The average time for the walk from Randa to the Weisshorn Hut—a vertical rise of 5500 feet—is four and a half hours, which would have meant arriving at dusk or even after dark. We climbed up through woods and pasturelands, using a slow and steady pace without any halts, and we arrived at the hut at six thirty, little more than three hours on the trail. The walk is a lovely one, to be enjoyed for itself. The terrain is varied, and the view is continuously superb. In front of us rose the mighty Zinal Rothorn. Across the valley, the incomparable Mischabel peaks—the Dom and Täschhorn and the five smaller peaks comprising the Nadelgrat.

The Weisshorn Hut is the smallest of the important huts in the Zermatt area, with accommodations for only twenty-eight and a hutkeeper in residence (at least this summer) only on weekends. Unlike the Matterhorn Hut, where a circus atmosphere prevails, this hut gives one a feeling of truly being in the mountains. The night we were there, there were seven others who planned to climb the mountain the next day (the first time that summer we would have company!), a half dozen others who had climbed the peak that day and preferred to get a night's rest at the hut before continuing down, and an altogether likable photographer who had made the tiring hike up in the hopes of getting some unusual high-altitude sunset and sunrise shots.

The next morning we were up at ten minutes to one and under way just an hour later, using our headlights in the darkness. The Weisshorn is higher than the Matterhorn and its hut is more than a thousand feet lower than the Matterhorn Hut. It is a long climb, and an early start is essential.

First we crossed the somewhat crevassed Schalli Glacier; then we climbed a gentle snow slope that gradually steepened. Next we tackled the huge rocky buttress leading up to the east ridge. We started off with immediate difficulties, but Rony, remembering that there should be no difficulties on this part of the climb, quickly got us on the proper route. In fact, it was more scrambling than real rock climbing. But it was long—very long. After four

The Weisshorn

hours, we finally reached the ridge, taking our first rest at the little depression in the ridge known as the Breakfast Place.

From there, the more serious climbing began, with a rock ridge bristling with some twenty little gendarmes. The first one is the famous "Lochmatter Gendarme," named for a renowned guide from St. Niklaus who fell to his death from this pinnacle some fifty years ago. The spiky tooth can be avoided by traversing dangerous loose rock to the right, but it is more sporting to climb it by the crest.

The key move involves a long stretch to a good handhold above on the left. I think you have to be six foot five or have abnormally long arms to make this move unassisted. The usual method is for the leader to step up on the back and shoulders of the second, thereby bringing the elusive handhold within reach. My body trembled as Rony's weight came down on it, but the pitch was successfully negotiated. The rest of the rock ridge provided amusing and highly exposed scrambling but no special difficulties. Soon we were starting the sharp snow ridge that gradually widens and steepens as it leads to the summit.

The Lyskamm and the Dent d'Hérens had been excellent training, and neither the exposure nor the steepness bothered me at all. Thanks to Rony's expert leadership, we overtook the other three ropes—all of whom had started well ahead of us—and were the first to climb up on the narrow pointed summit. The Weisshorn was ours!

It is a beautiful mountain from every direction, a dazzling pyramid whose three ridges melt into a narrow point, piercing the sky. Its faces are all steep, and you really do feel a little closer to heaven on that point. The day was perfect, and we spent close to an hour on the summit, drinking in the view, reminiscing about past climbs, and looking across the valley to the spiky ridge of the Nadelgrat, our next climb.

Our descent was unusually rapid, and we were back at the hut in little more than three hours. Then we ran down the vertical mile to Randa in seventy minutes—a new record for Rony and an all-out challenge to the shock absorbers in my legs!

After all the years of dreaming about the Weisshorn, the climb had seemed almost too easy. However, it wasn't the mountain, but other factors that made me feel that. We had enjoyed perfect conditions, always a key factor on any climb. Furthermore, I had made the climb after being in Zermatt for almost two months and was probably in the best shape of my life. In other summers, I would have had great difficulty in getting to the top, if I had made it at all. I was more convinced than ever that for most of the peaks around Zermatt, physical condition was perhaps the most important ingredient for an enjoyable as well as successful climb. When you are tired, everything seems steeper, more exposed, more difficult. When you are absolutely fit, most of the normal routes hold no special terrors.

Two days later I met one of the men who had climbed the Weisshorn the day I did; he told me that the day after our climb a man had suffered a broken arm when he was hit by a falling stone at the base of the Weisshorn's rocky buttress. Again, we don't conquer mountains. If we have good luck, we pass beautiful hours of intense struggle on their flanks and return uninjured to our normal habitat in the valleys, enriched by the experience.

Would we be lucky on the Nadelgrat? I couldn't put the gendarme-studded ridge out of my mind. The weather broke, and for two weeks an attempt on the ridge was unthinkable. I began to wonder if we would get a chance, if I was not getting too soft sitting in the village. And then, on August 21, the weather started to clear. On Thursday, August 24, we set out for the Bordier Hut and a go at the Nadelgrat.

In reality, our last "four thousander" was not a single peak, but five of them, connected to one another by a ridge that never drops below four thousand meters. Once up on the ridge, the vertical intervals aren't great, but the ridge is very long, continually sharp, narrow, and exposed. And there are literally countless pinnacles and spikes to cross during the traverse. Ordinarily, the so-called Nadelgrat consists of three peaks—the Sudlenz, the Nadelhorn, and the Stecknadelhorn. We intended to add the two northern outlying peaks, the Hohberghorn and the Dürrenhorn, to our itinerary. We had our first indication of the length of the trip when three guides from the mountain center of Pontresina arrived at the Bordier Hut at seven P.M., having covered our proposed route from the opposite direction. That was a little late to get down, but we assumed that they had gotten off to a late start. After all, guides would certainly move rapidly together, unencumbered by any tourists.

We were glad to meet up with Paul Julen, a popular Zermatt guide who, in company with one of his clients, planned to climb the Dürrenhorn, Hohberghorn, Stecknadelhorn, and Nadelhorn. We thought we would part company at the Nadelhorn, Paul and his client descending to the Mischabel Hut and Saas Fee while Rony and I continued over the Sudlenz and Lenzjoch before descending to the Dom Hut and Randa.

Sleep did not come easily that night. First there was a rousing chorus from a group of "seniors" enjoying a "high mountain touring week," and then a voluptuous fellow climber unabashedly changed her entire outfit while her ropemate held a light for her. The next day on the summit

of the Hohberghorn, Paul Julen admitted that he too had
enjoyed the show!

We got up at two thirty the next morning and at three
fifteen the four of us set out on what was to be the longest
day either Rony or I ever experienced. There was a full
moon, and the climb up to and across the Ried Glacier
was one of indescribable beauty. The glacier shimmered
in the moonlight, and the Nadelgrat directly in front of us
was highlighted in silver. Only the crunch of our boots
intruded on the silvery silence of this enchanted world.

Our first goal was to reach the Hohbergjoch, a depression in the ridge between the northernmost Dürrenhorn
and the Hohberghorn. As we reached the bottom of the
snow slope leading up to the col, the sun rose. The peaks
were lit in brilliant pinks and golds, and the moon was
still visible. We had expected to find an easy snow slope
and were quite surprised to find the gully leading up to
the Hohbergjoch was no less than fifty degrees!

The snow, however, was excellent and in the few icy
spots the guides from Pontresina had cut excellent steps.
Our progress was smooth, and in little more than four
hours from the Bordier Hut we were on our pass. We left
our rucksacks and climbed back toward the Dürrenhorn.
By eight o'clock we had bagged our first peak!

Back at the Hohbergjoch, we had a brief rest. Then
the four of us set out for the Hohberghorn, the longest
(about a thousand feet) vertical ascent once we had
gained the crest of the ridge. At first, the ridge was snowy,
wide, and easy. Near the top it became considerably
steeper and rocky. The rocks were iced up and in places
covered with snow. The climbing was distinctly delicate
here, but soon enough the top was reached, and we shook
hands all around on peak number two.

Another brief rest, and we were off again, descending
to the Stecknadeljoch and then along the spiky ridge that

runs from it to the Stecknadelhorn, the beginning of the actual Nadelgrat. Here, we got a taste of better things to come. While the Stecknadelhorn presents a spiky crest, most of the difficulties are easily circumvented by traversing a few meters below the crest on the west (Zermatt) side. The exposure is great, however, and the mixture of snow and rock is representative of the remainder of the climb.

After less than an hour's scrambling we were on top of the Stecknadelhorn. Here we met two parties who were traversing from the opposite direction, having started at the Dom Hut. We pressed on, eager to stand on our fourth peak—the Nadelhorn—and eat a well-deserved lunch of cold chicken, sausage, and cheese. As on the Hohberghorn, the lower part of the ridge was easy, but snow-covered blocks and boulders near the top necessitated delicate scrambling. By noon, we were there.

We were a little behind schedule, and I began to wonder if the day would be long enough for us to complete our climb. Paul and his client were preparing to descend. I knew the best climbing started at the Nadelhorn, but I nevertheless asked Rony if he thought we could do it. I admitted that I was a little bit tired after almost nine hour of climbing. Perhaps we should come back another time for the Sudlenz. Rony wouldn't hear of this. Totally confident in his own powers and our ability to see the climb to a successful conclusion, he pointed out that we were at an altitude greater than the summit of the Sudlenz. It would be a pity to climb all the way down to a hut and climb all the way up again. Besides, the weather was perfect, and another day . . . who knows?

I decided to use my remaining energy climbing rather than arguing with Rony, so we set off down the Nadelgrat to the Nadeljoch, a rocky island marking the low point on the ridge between the Nadelhorn and the Sudlenz. The guidebook had said this was the most enjoyable part of the climb—real rock climbing—and the book was right. There were huge blocks, slabs, cracks, chimneys, gullies. On the most difficult gendarme, a pinnacle of some fifteen to twenty feet, we had to use any slight roughness in the rock for pressing our fingers and toes against the slab. There was enough snow on this tower so that each move required sweeping snow before upward progress was possible. This was real climbing, not within the reach of every mortal!

Once the Nadeljoch was reached, after about an hour and a half's roller-coaster ride over the countless rock towers, the climbing changed dramatically. Now we were on a knife-edge snow ridge that made even the Lyskamm look wide! Halfway to the Sudlenz, a few rocks broke up the ridge. Then snow again. Then some steepish rocks. Finally, blue sky.

Tears streamed down my face. Rony understood and didn't say a word. It had taken fourteen years, but I had now stood on the summit of every one of the thirty-seven four-thousand-meter peaks surrounding Zermatt. It was getting late, but we lingered awhile. It was a great moment for both of us.

But we weren't exactly home yet. The spiky south ridge of the Sudlenz is steep loose rock and quite exposed. We descended quickly enough, until we were confronted by a seemingly impossible "characteristic" (guidebook terminology) gendarme. We tried to go around it, but wound up on an isolated crest, separated from the main ridge. We tried to cross a gully to get back to the main ridge, but the rotten snow avalanched the moment we touched it. Finally, just before desperation set in, we discovered the right route—a series of broken ledges just beneath the actual crest.

Up and down over the endless pinnacles and spires, we finally reached the Lenzjoch. Rotten snow at an angle of close to forty-five degrees made extreme caution necessary. Once the angle eased, we fairly ran down the easier slopes to the Festijoch and the Dom Hut. We were now involved in a race with the sun. We won, but barely, reaching the hut at eight P.M., almost seventeen hours after our start.

John Morton and staff members of his European Camp Association were waiting to celebrate with me that evening. And Stephanie was expecting Rony at home. Gluttons for punishment, we phoned from the hut and set off in the dark!

The Dom Hut walk is the steepest in the Valais, and descending it by headlight convinced us more than ever that this was more like climbing than hiking. The fixed cables attached to the steepest rocks made it somewhat safer, but we almost roped up again. At ten thirty we finaly emerged from the woods and tramped down the back streets of Randa.

The day still wasn't over. A few workmen in a café offered to give us a ride back to Zermatt when their card game was over. By eleven thirty, it was apparent that in their state of inebriation, a ride would be distinctly more dangerous than the Nadelgrat. In desperation, I phoned Zermatt, and Helmut Fraiss, the popular barman from the Post Hotel, said he would pick us up. Rony, so optimistic throughout the day, doubted that anyone would come for us at that hour. We could sleep in the fields and take the six A.M. train the next morning. As Rony started to remove his shoes, Helmut appeared. We couldn't believe we were actually on the last lap of our one-day Odyssey. At twelve thirty A.M. we were walking up Zermatt's main street, now deserted. We would celebrate our accomplishment, but not now. Sleep was what really mattered.

Sleep . . .

Chapter 17

Looking Backward and Forward

Having realized my second dream, I found myself feeling as I did after climbing the Matterhorn. What next? When you realize a dream, you lose it. The Matterhorn had been my childhood dream, the "four thousanders" the dream of my early manhood.

Today, my feelings are quite different. My goal is not a specific peak or group of peaks. Rather, it is to continue climbing—new routes around Zermatt, perhaps some mountains in the Bernese Oberland or the Engadine, perhaps out West in the Tetons or the Sierras. But the important thing is the joy of climbing in and of itself, and the special quality of friendship in the mountains. At this point, I get as much pleasure—albeit a different kind—from introducing friends to the high mountains as I do from "bagging" a new peak. Hiking in New Hampshire's White Mountains is more enjoyable than ever when I am with a congenial group of mountain lovers.

More than ever before, to me the mountains are a great place to get to know yourself and your friends. In an increasingly complex age, they provide the ideal setting for a return to simplicity. Mountain climbing and trail walking may be escapes, but lessons can be learned during these escapes that are transferable to real life. Friendships are begun and strengthened. Cooperation is built through the interdependence of a group of friends. Then, one's self-confidence is heightened through accomplishment; patience is rewarded; and an awareness of one's own abilities and limitations is sharpened.

Climbing is more than a sport. I won't call it a way of life. Other than mountain guides and ski instructors, few of us can earn our living from the mountains. But they can influence our way of life, our system of values.

As indicated earlier, you do not need to be a superman to enjoy the mountains. The more you give, the more you will receive from them. Whether your ultimate goal is Mount Everest, the Matterhorn, or a local hill, the mountains will provide you with an unequaled playground. It doesn't matter whether you become a rock specialist, or an expert in ice climbing, or a devotee of local trails, flowers, wildlife. The mountains are there, ready to welcome you, provided you show them the proper respect.

There are organizations ready to help pave the way to this special world of the mountains. The most important thing is to start with a positive attitude and avoid biting off more than you can chew. Any person in reasonably good health can enjoy the mountains. The better shape you're in, the more you can do in the hills, but how much you do will depend on your motivation. Anyway, it's not the quantity that counts, but the quality of the experience, in turn dependent on your attitude. I've seen hikers get far more joy from a tramp in the White Mountains than many a Matterhorn conqueror.

There is a little bit of the bear who "went over the mountain" in all of us. There is a feeling of elation when we gaze down on the world we know from above. The astronauts have taken the ultimate "trip"; for the rest of us, climbing provides a way to rise above our daily routines while still keeping both feet on the ground!

If you will take the first upward step, a beautiful world awaits you. Mountains are for mortals . . . for all of us!

Appendix

How you go about your apprenticeship will be all-important in your development as a mountaineer. It has been a source of considerable pain for me to watch neophytes in the hands of teachers more intent on impressing with their own skills than assuring the happy introduction of the newcomer to the sport. The result all too often is disappointment, from which the novice retreats—never to return. Unlike most sports, where to exceed your limits means nothing more than walking off the field, court, or gym floor, mountaineering can engender great fear when the climber tries something that is too hard.

There are organizations that can help you during your apprenticeship. I have listed a variety of these organizations both in America and in Europe, which may directly assist the climber or else direct him to the nearest help. My thanks to the American Alpine Club for its help in this compilation.

Major American Climbing Schools

Bob Culp Climbing School
P.O. Box 3034
Boulder, Colorado 80303

Jackson Hole Mountain Guides, Inc.
P.O. Box 193
Teton Village, Wyoming 83025

Rainier Mountaineering, Inc.
Whittaker's Chalet
3801 South Steele
Tacoma, Washington 98409

Royal Robbins' Rockcraft
906 Durant
Modesto, California 95350

Glenn Exum Guide Service
Grand Teton National Park
Moose, Wyoming 83012

Mountain Travel (USA)
62101 Medau Place
Oakland, California 94611

North American Mountaineering
% Eastern Mountain Sports
1041 Commonwealth Avenue
Boston, Massachusetts 02215

Yosemite Mountaineering School
Yosemite Park & Curry Co.
Yosemite National Park, California 95389

Lute Jerstad Adventures
9920 S.W. Terwilliger Boulevard
Portland, Oregon 97219

European Alpine Clubs

AUSTRIA
Osterreichischen Alpenclub
Getreidemarkt 3/II
1060 Wien

BELGIUM
Club Alpin Belge
37 Sq. Ambiorix
1049 Bruxelles

CZECHOSLOVAKIA
Czechoslovak Mountain Union
Na Porici 12
Praha 1

ENGLAND
The Alpine Club
74 Audley Street
London W.1Y

Austrian Alpine Club
26 Old Bond Street
London W.1

FRANCE
Club Alpin Français
7 rue La Boetie
Paris 8e

Sections Rhône-Alpes
Club Alpin Français
38 rue Thomassin
Lyon 2

GREECE
Hellenic Alpine Club
18 rue Phidiou
Athens 142

ITALY
Club Alpino Italiano
Sezione de Milano
via U. Foscolo 3
20121 Milano

POLAND
Klubu Wysokogorskiego
ul. Sienkiewicza 12, p. 439
Warszawa 36

SPAIN
Club Alpino Español
Mayor 6
Madrid

SWITZERLAND
Club Alpin Suisse
rue Beau-Séjour 24
1003 Lausanne

WEST GERMANY
Deutscher Alpenverein
Sektion Berlin
Hauptstrasse 23-24
1000 Berlin 62

Deutscher Alpenverein
Sektion Stuttgart
Marienstrasse 5 V
Stuttgart S

YUGOSLAVIA
Planinske Aveza Slovenije
p.p. 214
61001 Ljubljana

Union International des Associations d'Alpinisme
29, rue des Délices
1211 Génève I
Switzerland

The American Alpine Club has eight sections, located in Alaska, Colorado, Los Angeles, New England, New York, Oregon, San Francisco, and Washington. Headquarters, including the 7500-volume library and the Alpine Museum, are at 113 East 90 Street, New York, New York 10028. While the American Alpine Club does not sponsor weekend outings or teach climbing, there are numerous regional mountain clubs that do. Among the largest and best organized are:

Appalachian Mountain Club, 5 Joy Street, Boston, Massachusetts 02108 (Northeast coast, with chapters in Pennsylvania, New York, and the New England states)

Colorado Mountain Club, 1723 East 16 Avenue, Denver, Colorado 80218 (covers the Rockies in general)

Iowa Mountaineers, P.O. Box 163, Iowa City, Iowa 52240

Mazamas, 909 N.W. 19 Street, Portland, Oregon 97209

The Mountaineers, P.O. Box 122, Seattle, Washington 98111 (active in Washington and Oregon)

Potomac Appalachian Trail Club, 1718 N. Street, N.W., Washington, D.C. 20336 (Virginia, West Virginia, Maryland, and the District of Columbia)

Sierra Club, 1050 Mills Tower, San Francisco, California 94104 (chapters throughout the United States)

While the above lists are not intended to be complete, they should give you a fairly good idea of how and where to get started.

The important point is to set some kind of short-term goals for yourself, taking into consideration your physical abilities as well as your motivation. The fact that you do not want to become a "human monkey," scaling vertical or near-vertical rock walls, does not rule out the high mountains for you. There are many beautiful peaks, both at home and abroad, which involve long but easy ascents over relatively gentle snow slopes. And many of the more celebrated rock peaks have "tourist routes" that are easier than most of the routes on local training rocks and quarries.

Most of the organizations listed above have programs for climbers of all levels of ability. As I said in the introduction, you don't have to be a champion to enjoy the sport! All of these organizations will be in a position to give you advice on equipment, both basic and supplementary. If there aren't any appropriate stores near where you live, there are a number of outstanding manufacturers and distributors operating catalog businesses that will send you what you require through the mail.

There are also numerous publications that range in their interests from the coverage of new climbs to the latest developments in equipment. *Backpacker, Ascent, Summit,* and *Better Camping* are a few among a rapidly expanding list. In addition, many of the clubs listed above put out an annual or even quarterly publication that often goes well beyond the immediate activities of the club. Indeed, the sport seems to have inspired a whole subculture!